Superior Test Preparation Presents:

The ACT Test: Power Preparation 2013 – 2014

Nicholas A. LaMantia

Copyright ©2013 Nicholas A. LaMantia / Superior Test Preparation
All Rights Reserved. No part of this publication can be reproduced or transmitted without permission in writing from Superior Test Preparation.

ACTPowerPrep.com **SuperiorTestPrep.com**

ACT® is the registered trademark of ACT, Inc.
Nicholas LaMantia and Superior Test Preparation have no affiliation with ACT, Inc.
All statements regarding ACT policy reflect the rules at the time of publication. The author and Superior Test Preparation are not responsible for events occurring due to a change in ACT policy.

Table of Contents

Introduction and ACT Test FAQ	3
How to Use *The ACT Test: Power Preparation*	8
General ACT Tips	9
Section 1 – Tips, Tricks, and Strategies	
Chapter 1 – English	10
Chapter 2 – Math	27
Chapter 3 – Reading	57
Chapter 4 – Science	84
Chapter 5 – Writing	101
Section 2 – Answer Explanations to ACT Test 64E*	
Introduction	113
English	114
Math	121
Reading	141
Science	153

*A link to ACT Test form 64E is available at ACTPowerPrep.com

Introduction and ACT Test FAQ

The ACT test has worried students for over 50 years now. One test with so much on the line can be quite nerve-wracking, right? Well you can worry about it a little – that's only healthy – but there is no need to freak out. First of all, your high school grades and classes will be the most important part of your college applications, so keep working away in the classroom. Secondly, the ACT can be taken as many times as you wish, and at the current rate of $36.50 per test (the optional writing adds $16 more), it is not all that expensive to give it another go. Finally, through practice and good advice, anyone can earn a solid score on the ACT. Relax and do your best.

Some common questions students have about the ACT Test:

What will I be tested on? How long does the testing take?

The ACT is a multiple choice test with four separate sections called "subtests." The four subtests are labeled English, Math, Reading, and Science. Each subtest has a time limit of between 35 and 60 minutes. Overall you will be taking about three hours of tests, but the whole process takes about four hours including breaks and the reading of directions. You may also take the optional Writing Test, which is a 30 minute test given about 15 minutes after the four subtests are completed.

When is the test offered and how do I sign up?

ACT offers one national test day each February, April, June, September, October, and December. Additionally, some states organize a statewide test day for high school juniors to take the ACT during school hours. The statewide tests are usually administered in March or April.

The sign up deadline for a national test day is roughly a month before the day of the exam. See *actstudent.org* for exact schedules. You can register late (up to about three weeks before test time), but you will be required to pay an extra fee. Registration for the statewide test day is generally handled by your high school.

What is the story with the optional Writing Test? Should I take it?

The optional Writing Test gives you 30 minutes to compose a written response to a question or "prompt" chosen by ACT. You will not know the prompt until you begin the test, but the subject of the prompt always is relevant to a high school student. More detailed information on the format and scoring of the Writing Test can be found on pages 101 – 103 of this book.

You probably should take the optional Writing Test. Chances are at least one college on your list either recommends or requires it. You can check *actstudent.org/writing* or the official college website to find a specific university's policy for the Writing Test. Even if your college choices don't require the test, it still shows good initiative to take Writing. Plus, by studying this book and practicing, you should have no problem getting a decent score, even if writing is not your strongest subject.

What is the scoring scale for the ACT? What is a good score?

The four subtests of the ACT are each graded on a 1 – 36 scale, with 36 being the best possible score. You also receive a composite score, which averages the scores of your four subtests into one overall score on a 1 – 36 scale. The national average for the composite score is roughly a 21.

Although this may sound cheesy, a "good score" is the score you receive when you perform to the best of your own abilities. If you got a 28, but did not prepare for the test and stayed out late the night before taking it, you really did not get a good score. With a little hard work you could have scored in the 30s and put yourself in line for scholarship money. If you got a 19, but worked hard to prepare for the test, then you did get a good score. Maybe you improved from a 16 and now can attend a four year university instead of the local community college.

How are the individual subtests graded?

You receive a score based solely on the number of questions you get correct. No extra penalty is assessed for incorrect answers, so don't leave anything blank. The exact grading scale changes slightly from test to test because every test has its own curve. For example, on an easier test you may get 45 questions correct on the Math section and receive a 25. On a harder test, 45 questions correct might be scored as a 27.

How is my composite (overall) score determined?

Your composite score is determined by averaging the scores you receive on each of the four subtests (English, Math, Reading, and Science). The Writing score and the Writing / English score do not affect your composite score at all. These scores are presented in addition to the composite if you choose to take the Writing Test.

The test was harder / easier than the practice exam. What gives?

Every test is different. Sometimes the Reading section is a breeze, and sometimes it is full of complicated language. Sometimes you don't see any advanced trigonometry in the

Math section; sometimes you see three questions on it. It's the luck of the draw. Just remember, it's all graded on a curve, so harder tests mean easier grading standards.

I heard it's easier to get a high score on the September / April / June / etc. test. Is that true?

No test is easier to score well on than the others. ACT designs all their test forms to cover the same skills and knowledge. Since it is impossible to make all tests of identical difficulty, the grading curves are then designed to make every test equal.

Although the test itself is no different, it usually is best to take the ACT near the end of 11th grade (the April and June exams). You should also take an exam prior to that (the December and/or February exam) to get familiar with the testing process. It is OK to take the exam in the beginning of 12th grade (the September and October exams), but that should be a fallback if things didn't go well on your first couple tries.

How many times should I take the test?

Take the test two to four times. Nearly 60% percent of students see a rise in their score from their first to second test. And if your score stays the same or drops, no big deal, <u>you only need to report your best score to colleges anyway</u>. If you are happy with your score after your second try, that's good enough. If you think you can do better or are shooting for a scholarship or 'reach school,' try it a third or fourth time. Taking it five or more times is fine, but you will probably not make any significant gains by then.

What is superscoring?

Recently, some colleges have started to 'superscore' the ACT Test. This means the college takes the highest individual subject test scores from all the ACT Tests you have taken. For example, say in December you got the following scores: 30 English / 25 Math / 25 Reading / 24 Science. Then in February you got these scores: 28 English / 27 Math / 28 Reading / 23 Science. A 'superscoring' school would take the English and Science scores from your first test and the Math and Reading scores from your second test. When a university superscores, you definitely want to take the test multiple times. Consult the official college website to find a specific university's policy on the ACT.

Can I get my answer / question sheet back?

For certain national test days, you can pay $19 for a "Test Information Release (TIR)." The TIR includes a copy of the questions, your answers, and the correct answers. Lately, this service is only offered for the December, April, and June tests. Check *actstudent.org/scores/release.html* for specific details. <u>If you think you may take the ACT</u>

again at some point, order the TIR. It is very helpful to review your test, go over questions you missed, and determine the areas in which you need more practice. Your TIR can be ordered through *actstudent.org* during registration or up to three months after the test day.

Note: A good start to your ACT preparation is to take the December exam and order the TIR (while in 11th grade). This will provide some information about where you stand and where improvements are necessary. Then you can begin studying for the April and June tests.

How many correct answers do I need for a certain score?

Again, it depends on the curve. Generally, for every one or two questions you miss on a section you lose a point. Here are a few figures from the official scoring of a recent ACT Test to give you an idea:

English – 75 questions total
70 correct = 32 ; 65 correct = 27 ; 55 correct = 22 ; 45 correct = 19 ; 35 correct = 15

Math – 60 questions total
55 correct = 32 ; 50 correct = 28 ; 40 correct = 24 ; 30 correct = 19 ; 20 correct = 16

Reading – 40 questions total
35 correct = 31 ; 30 correct = 26 ; 25 correct = 22 ; 20 correct = 18 ; 15 correct = 14

Science – 40 questions total
35 correct = 30 ; 30 correct = 26 ; 25 correct = 23 ; 20 correct = 20 ; 15 correct = 17

All four tests were of normal difficulty, so these are close to average numbers. The exact scale fluctuates slightly from test to test, but the numbers will always be similar to these.

I took the test already, but now I want my composite score to go up two points. What do I need to do?

You will need to get about 9 – 18 more questions correct throughout the entire test. Remember that your composite score is the average of your four scores on the subtests. If you work hard to bring your Math score up four points, but all your other scores stay the same, your composite score only rises one point. Be well-rounded and work on every section, whether it is a strength or a weakness. The goal is simply to get more questions correct!

Note: Sometimes it's easier to gain points on your best tests than it is to gain points on your worst tests. For example, turning a 25 into a 28 can be easier than turning a 19 into a 22.

How do I send scores to colleges? Can I select which scores I report from different test days?

First of all, you cannot send certain sections from certain days. You have to send the entire ACT score report for a given day. With that said, if in October you got a 17 overall and in April you got a 21, you do not need to tell the college your October score. Send only the April report. You can send official reports to colleges through the ACT website. You can also arrange to have reports automatically sent to colleges when you register for the test. However, with this option you will not be able to see your score before the college does, so I do not recommend it.

Note: If you have other questions regarding the basics of the ACT, log on to www.actstudent.org/FAQ. It contains official information about registering for the test, score reporting, special accommodations, and more.

How to Use *The ACT Test: Power Preparation*

First of all, I recommend that you supplement this book with at least two practice tests (three to five tests would be best). This book has many practice questions, but it is more of a strategy guide. **Sitting down and taking complete tests is extremely helpful.** Practice test books are inexpensive online or at book stores, and they often are available at your school or local library for free. I strongly recommend practice tests from ACT, Inc (the creators of the ACT Test), which are most readily found in the *Real ACT* book.

ACTPowerPrep.com **contains a link to practice test 64E, an official test from ACT, Inc. Answers and explanations to all the questions on test 64E are found in the back of this book** (beginning on page 113). Another free practice test from ACT, Inc. is available at ***ACTstudent.org/sampletest***. The site also provides answers and brief explanations for each question. After studying this book and completing a few practice tests, you will be completely prepared for the ACT.

The key to getting the most from your ACT study time (or any study time) is a concept I call 'Active Preparation.' Active Preparation does not mean you must spend months studying for the ACT. Actually, roughly 20 – 40 hours of total preparation time should be adequate. Active Preparation simply means that your brain is constantly working during your study time; it is making connections and intently trying to learn new concepts. Active Preparation is psychologically proven to be more effective than simply trying to memorize. Results come quickly with an 'active' approach.

So how does *The ACT Test: Power Preparation* fit into Active Preparation? *Power Preparation* is short, but loaded with strategies. When I tutor students, I go over the strategies in this book many times. Consequently, this book is not designed to be read once and put away. Read through it slowly and highlight passages you find especially helpful. Write down notes and always be thinking of ways you can apply the tricks and tips to test questions. As you correct practice tests, keep this book open and find connections between the practice questions and the tips from this book. Finally, review this book and any notes you have as your test date approaches.

When reviewing practice tests, the concept of Active Preparation also comes into play. 'Actively' correct practice problems and previous ACT Tests you have taken. Don't just mark something wrong and move on. Study the correct answer and try to understand why you got the question wrong. Learn from your mistakes so you do not make them again on the next test.

Analyzing a practice test you took is a much better way to spend a couple of hours than just mindlessly moving on to another test. The goal is to learn something!

General ACT Tips – A Few Pointers to Use throughout the Test

- Don't leave anything blank! Your score is determined solely by the number of questions you answer correctly. There is no penalty for wrong answers.

- Don't spend too much time on any one question. **Every question, hard or easy, is worth the same amount of points.** If you are struggling with a question, circle it and come back at the end if you have time. You don't want to miss the last five questions because you wasted time on one really tough one.

- When you are working on a question, cross out answers that you're sure are incorrect. Narrowing things down clears your thinking and improves your chances when making a guess.

- Follow the advice in this book, but also use your brain. Not every question will fit squarely into one of this book's tips and tricks. You have been going to school and taking tests for many years; use that knowledge as well!

- Be prepared. This doesn't mean you need to study for months or spend hundreds on tutoring. Simply knowing the test format and having a strategy going into the test will improve your score considerably.

- Be in peak condition on test day. Stay in and get some rest the night before the test. Eat a solid breakfast of carbohydrate and protein-rich foods (sugary foods can make you crash midway through the test). Have pencils and calculators ready to go. Being prepared calms your nerves and gives you confidence.

- Stay calm and cool. Panicking because of pressure or lack of time will not help anything. Remember, you can always retake the test if things go wrong.

Chapter 1 – English

English is probably the easiest section to improve upon, so spend some time working on it. If you have never taken an ACT English Test, try at least two passages from a practice test before getting into the "Tips, Tricks, and Strategies" section on page 11. The free test available at *ACTstudent.org/sampletest* will work fine.

Format and Basic Strategy

The ACT English Test focuses on grammar, sentence structure, and general organization. The English Test contains five short passages, each with 15 questions interspersed throughout the text. The questions and passages are in no specific order; you will find all the passages have a similar level of difficulty.

You have 45 minutes to complete the 75 questions, which means you must average 36 seconds per question or less. This sounds short, but these questions generally do not take long to complete. Practice and find a comfortable pace for yourself – you probably have more time than you think.

The format for most questions is that ACT underlines part of a passage and then expects you to correct any errors made. Here's a quick example to illustrate the format:

Jim went to Puerto <u>Rico; for the first time, in</u> 1935.

A. NO CHANGE
B. Rico, for the first time in
C. Rico for the first time in
D. Rico for the first time, in

"NO CHANGE" means that you are choosing to leave the text as it is. The correct answer is C.

Some questions will give further directions besides just looking at the underlined part of the passage. I refer to these as 'verbal questions' because they actually ask a question in words. For example, a 'verbal question' may look like this:

Which statement best expands on the information in the previous sentence?

A. Jim once went to Alaska.
B. Many people prefer deserts to islands.
C. Jim was born in 1870
D. Jim's trip to the island was the highlight of his year.

The correct answer is D (using the first example as the "previous sentence").

English Tips, Tricks, and Strategies

1. ***Read Everything***

    Unless you have major problems with finishing the English Test on time, it is best to read the entire passage as you go along. It is tempting to skip sentences that do not have questions in them, but you will perform better overall if you read them anyway. Reading everything enables you to understand the content and flow of the passage, which is helpful on many questions.

2. ***Go with the Simplest Answer***

    If the simplest answer fits in the sentence, go with it. The ACT constantly asks questions that test your ability to keep text brief and to the point. For students who are in the 16 – 20 range in English, this tip alone can bring a score to the low 20s. For those who are strong in English, just keep this tip in mind; it is extremely useful. Here are a few examples to illustrate this tip:

    We sat on the plane, eager to start our long flight <u>north, a lengthy journey.</u>

    A. NO CHANGE
    B. north, a long tour.
    C. north in the jet.
    D. north.

The correct answer is D. The sentence already mentioned that it is a long flight in a plane. We don't need to say that it is lengthy or in a jet again. **Never add extra words unless they present genuinely new and important information.** The ACT constantly tries to trick you into repeating information or adding irrelevant ideas. If you are unsure about an answer, opt to keep the text brief and simple. About 85% of the time ACT wants you to remove words, not add them.

    The farmer makes both pies from the fruit and strong, durable clothing from the stalk <u>is made also.</u>

    A. NO CHANGE
    B. is made.
    C. is also made.
    D. DELETE the underlined text (and place a period at the end of the sentence).

The correct answer is D. The sentence already said "the farmer makes both," so the underlined text is basically repeating information that has already been mentioned. The sentence sounds perfectly fine after deleting the text (it actually makes it a bit smoother), so we keep things short and simple.

Note: In the last example, it may have been easier to read if you removed the words "strong" and "durable" from the sentence. If you are unsure about an answer, try ignoring any extra descriptive words. The basics of the sentence will not change, and it can make it easier to pick up on the flow of the text.

    My team <u>succeeded, we</u> won the semi-final.

    A. NO CHANGE
    B. succeeded. We
    C. succeeded we
    D. succeeded then we

The correct answer is B. This example uses the *Go with the Simplest Answer* tip in a different way than just eliminating extra text. The simplest method to connect thoughts is by adding a period and forming two sentences. If you can separate the original sentence into two simple sentences that make sense, it will always be correct.

    Jenny plays piano better than anyone I have ever seen. <u>Therefore, she</u> misses notes sometimes.

    A. NO CHANGE
    B. Meanwhile,
    C. Even she, however,
    D. She

The correct answer is C. As I mentioned, the shortest answer is not right 100% of the time. Occasionally we need to add words so the text is grammatically correct and readable. Here we must add "Even she, however," because it helps the two sentences fit together. Choice D (the shortest) would basically say, 'She is the best. She messes up.' That does not make much sense.

Note: The previous example further illustrates Tip #1 (Read Everything). If you were not paying attention to the content of the passage, you easily could have chosen the wrong answer.

3. ***Read the Whole Sentence before Answering the Question***

    Many students read up to the underlined portion of the sentence, answer the question, and completely forget about the rest of the sentence. This is a common mistake. Sometimes an answer seems correct halfway through a sentence, but becomes wrong when the rest of the thought is taken into account. **Read the whole sentence before choosing an answer.** In fact, if you are unsure of the answer, try inserting each choice into the sentence and reading the result from start to finish. The following examples illustrate this tip.

The design worked <u>well as</u> he created his first guitar – and his young life's dream – he knew his grandpa was proud.

A. NO CHANGE
B. well, as
C. well. As
D. well,

The correct answer is C. Only by reading all the way through to the period can you understand why this must be separated into two sentences. Remember, separating it into two complete sentences is always preferable to using commas.

The <u>author was</u> James Joyce, born in 1882 to wealthy parents in the Dublin suburb of Rathgar.

A. NO CHANGE
B. author,
C. author, who went by the name
D. author

The correct answer is A. Many students choose B because it looks like it fits best at first sight. But if we read the entire sentence, B sounds awkward (there is no verb!). Choice A gives a nice, full thought. We can only see that by reading the full sentence.

Note: Some of these examples may have been easy for you, but they can be much harder to recognize when in the middle of a long passage. Stay Alert!

4. ***Don't get Carried Away with the Commas***

On the ACT, students tend to use too many commas. If you are unsure about a comma, chances are one <u>should not</u> be used. This tip is especially helpful to those who score under 25 in English, but check it out either way, as it leads into the next tip.

In the more than <u>six weeks since</u> I started my paper route, my bike has not stalled once.

A. NO CHANGE
B. six, weeks since
C. six weeks, since
D. six weeks since,

As you probably guessed, the correct answer is A. A comma is simply a pause in speech. The underlined area sounds best if it flows without any pauses.

Note: Notice the comma after the word "route" in the previous example. You could say this sentence with or without a pause in that spot, so it would also be grammatically correct if no comma was there.

A quick word about commas: There are many grammatical rules about comma usage. Other than a few of these rules (which I cover later), you do not need to know them for the ACT. **For the purpose of the ACT, just think of a comma as a pause in speech.** *If you would like to learn the grammatical rules, simply Google™ "comma rules" and you will find many sites explaining them. My favorite is the "grammar.ccc" site that will be near the top of the search results. But be careful – often times the rules confuse you more than they help! Just thinking of commas as pauses is the most effective method.*

5. **Pretend you are Saying the Sentence to a Friend**

   This is one of the most simple, yet powerful tips for the ACT English Test. **The easiest way to answer many questions is simply to write the sentence the same way you would say it out loud.** Our first example of this was on the previous page. To determine comma usage, simply say the sentence out loud and put a comma in any place you paused.

   While this tip works well with comma questions, it can also be used on just about any question on the test. As you attempt to solve the following example, pretend you are saying the answer choices out loud to a friend and determine which sounds the best.

   > Even prior to 1920, there were scientific plans for television sets, but <u>that</u> took nearly 20 years until a commercial product reached stores.
   >
   > A. NO CHANGE
   > B. it
   > C. these
   > D. DELETE the underlined text.

   The correct answer is B. Choice B simply sounds the best when you read the sentence with each of the four options. Many students are tempted to choose C, but it sounds awkward when you say the sentence aloud with "these" in it.

   Grammar Note: Choice C is also grammatically incorrect. If "these" is referring back to the scientific plans, the end of the sentence would basically say, 'but scientific plans took nearly 20 years until a product reached stores.' That would not make sense at all.

6. **Be Literal – Answer Only the Question they Ask**

   This tip applies only to 'verbal questions' (see page 10 for a definition). You see at least 15 of these per test, and many students struggle with them. **The trick to these questions is to answer EXACTLY what is asked. Forget about all the other tips and tricks.**

Forget about what answer you think sounds best. Just answer the question. This is best illustrated through the following examples.

The Great Barrier Reef measures over 100,000 square miles. Its waters contain over 1500 species of fish.

> Given that all the choices are true, which sentence gives the most visual information about the reef environment?
>
> A. NO CHANGE
> B. The reef is located on the Northeast coast of Australia.
> C. Rows of multicolored plant and animal life stretch throughout the reef.
> D. Scuba divers can hardly believe their eyes when they first see the reef.

The correct answer is C. We wanted visual information about the reef environment, and C provides just that. ACT often tries to trick you with options like choice D. It talks about seeing the reef, but it does not really give any visual information about the reef itself.

The climate of California's coastline varies from the mild north to the hot southern tip of the state. The northwest contains more forests and wooded areas than the south.

> Given that all the choices are true, which sentence provides the most specific support for the preceding sentence? ("preceding sentence" = the sentence before this one)
>
> A. NO CHANGE
> B. Summer highs in Los Angeles (Southern CA) reach around 85° F, while San Francisco (Northern CA) only hits roughly 70° F.
> C. The Southern coast is a great place for surfing and water sports.
> D. My favorite city in California is San Diego.

The correct answer is B. This sentence may not sound the best at first, but remember, we are answering ONLY what the question asks. ACT wants specific support for the preceding sentence, which focuses on climate differences within California. Answer B gives specific information which directly supports the preceding sentence.

Note: You can take this approach to solve any 'verbal question.' Just remember your job is to answer ONLY what the question asks. These questions are not designed to test grammar or to have you determine which sentence sounds best.

The previous example also leads into my next tip...

7. *Don't Answer Questions Until You Have All the Information*

When in doubt read more; you will get a better understanding of the context (the background information) for the question. In the last example they wanted support for the previous sentence – if you did not reread the previous sentence you would be in trouble. Many different kinds of questions require additional reading; here is a list of the most common question types that may require extra reading:

- Figuring out tense (past, present, future, etc.)

    Is it 'Joe went to the doctor' or 'Joe is going to the doctor'? They are both grammatically correct. It would be essential to look at nearby sentences to figure out the correct tense for the verb.

- "Which best leads into the next paragraph"

    Sometimes ACT asks "Which sentence best leads into the next paragraph?" or "Which sentence best leads into the rest of the passage?" To answer these accurately, you must read or skim ahead to see what is coming up in the text. Some students like to skip these questions and save them until they finish the required reading.

- End of the passage questions

    Sometimes the last question of a passage will ask a broad question about everything you just read. Don't be afraid to go back and review the passage if necessary.

- Transition words – *this one is best illustrated through examples*

    Josh came down with the flu. However, he will miss the boating trip this year.

    A. NO CHANGE
    B. Conversely,
    C. Although,
    D. Thus,

The correct answer is D. The word "thus" means *as a result*, so it connects these two sentences well – 'He is sick. As a result, he cannot go boating.' Now look at it this way:

Josh is an expert sailor. However, he will miss the boating trip this year.

A. NO CHANGE
B. Conversely,
C. Therefore,
D. Thus,

The correct answer is A. The word "however" connects conflicting thoughts. It says, 'Even though Josh is an expert, he will not be able to make it this year.' "Therefore" and "thus" both function the opposite way; they connect thoughts that agree. "Conversely" is too strong a word and just does not sound right in this situation.

He was proud of his work. <u>Therefore,</u> his findings will save the company millions.

A. NO CHANGE
B. Although,
C. In spite of it,
D. DELETE the underlined text (and capitalize accordingly)

The correct answer is D. The transition words in choices A, B, and C do not help the flow of the text. Remember that ACT likes things short and simple; don't add words unless they are necessary.

The lesson: Which transition word(s) you use completely depends on the preceding sentence. You must read back and find the right word to connect the two thoughts.

8. **Go with Safer Answers**

When you correct the errors on the ACT English Test, do not try to turn the essay into a masterpiece of writing. The goal is to make it a nice, tight, easy-reading essay that is grammatically correct. **If you are picking between a big fancy word or phrase and a nice simple one that flows well, go with the simple one.**

Note: Take practice tests to get comfortable with all of these concepts.

Other ACT English Question Types

1. ***Order Questions***

    Each ACT contains roughly one to three questions asking if the order of sentences or paragraphs should be changed to improve the passage. These questions <u>always</u> have some distinct clue to the correct answer. Often it's as simple as putting things in chronological order (for example, move the sentence about 1984 before the sentence about 1987), but sometimes you have to look deeper. Take a little extra time on 'order questions.' Read as much as necessary and look for a clear reason for the sequence of sentences or paragraphs.

2. ***Which one is NOT or LEAST Acceptable Questions***

    Each ACT contains roughly four to seven questions that ask for an incorrect answer. My first advice on these is simply to watch out for them! Thousands of students each year get these questions wrong because they don't notice that they are supposed to choose the <u>incorrect</u> answer. Always read directions! In addition, take the time to look at all four answer choices when completing 'NOT or LEAST acceptable questions.' Sometimes a couple of answer choices don't sound great, but there is always just one choice that is completely unacceptable.

    These questions generally involve word choice, grammar, or context.

    - Word Choice: You get a list of four words and have to pick the one that would not work. Just remember that ACT prefers safe, easy-reading answers. They do not want you to turn the essay into a 'masterpiece' with unnecessarily fancy and confusing vocabulary.

    - Grammar: One of the four answers will simply be grammatically incorrect. Study the grammar rules in the next section and always correct your practice tests to stay sharp on grammar.

    - Context: Always try to follow along with what is happening in the passage. Sometimes all four answers are fine grammatically, but one answer is saying something that would not make sense in the context of the passage.

3. ***What Would Happen if you Deleted… Questions***

   Each ACT contains roughly one to three questions like this example:

   The student was celebrating a major accomplishment: the completion of his third semester at college.

   If the writer were to delete the phrase "his third semester at" from the preceding sentence, the paragraph would primarily lose information that:

   A. says that he will graduate college in a few years
   B. gives proof that he will begin his next semester shortly
   C. clarifies that only part of his college education is completed
   D. gives the idea that he preferred high school

   The correct answer is C. The best way to complete questions like this one is with a simple technique: first read the complete sentence, and then read it again without the deleted phrase. For this example, if we read the sentence without the phrase "his third semester at," it sounds like the student has completely finished college. The phrase lets us know that he has only finished a few semesters, so the answer is C. The other answer choices assume things that were not said. For example, choice B is probably true, but we don't know this for a fact. Maybe he is planning on taking some time off and isn't starting his next semester for a while. **Don't be creative or assume things on the English Test. Don't infer anything that is not plainly stated.**

4. ***Kept / Deleted and Yes / No Questions***

   Each ACT contains roughly two to five questions asking if a certain sentence or phrase should be included in the essay. Your job is to indicate whether the text should remain in the essay or be taken out, and to explain the reason for keeping/deleting it. As with all English Test questions you have four options; on these questions, two options involve keeping the text in the essay, and two involve deleting it. These questions require three skills: reading and understanding the essay (page 11), reading extra if necessary (page 15), and not making inferences (page 19). In addition, it is also extra important to read the question carefully. If you understand the question, know the content of the passage, and do not make assumptions, 'Yes / No' and 'Kept / Deleted' questions are no problem.

   Note: You will occasionally see other variations of 'verbal questions.' As long as you follow along with the content of the passage, read ahead when necessary, and strictly follow Tip #6, "Be Literal" (see page 14), these questions are not nearly as hard as they look. Also, as always, practice will improve your skills.

   Note: Examples of all these question types can be found on any ACT English Test.

Important Grammar Rules for the ACT English Test

- **Commas (,)**

    As mentioned earlier in this section, the best way to think of a comma is simply as a pause in speech. It is helpful to know a few grammar rules about them, though.

    o **The Double Comma**

    Sometimes two commas are used when extra information is added to a sentence.

    Berlin, the capital of Germany, is a fascinating city.

Notice how we could have just said, 'Berlin is a fascinating city.' We put two commas around the extra statement added in the middle of the sentence.

    He is a quarterback that, despite his weak arm, always throws accurately.

Again, we just added the bit about the weak arm. The rest of the sentence worked fine without it, so we put commas on either side.

    I like ketchup. I don't like tomatoes, though, and I will never eat one again.

The word "though" was not necessary to this sentence. Since it was just added into the middle of the thought, we put commas on either side. The 'double comma' can be tricky; it is the only case on the ACT in which treating a comma like a pause may not work perfectly.

    o **No Commas Between Complete Sentences**

    Never put a comma between complete sentences. If you can use a period (or semicolon), use it. If a period does work, a comma cannot be used.

    It was 1969, Buzz Aldrin had just completed the first moonwalk.

The above example is incorrect. Even though it is very short, "It was 1969" is a complete sentence. A period or semicolon would be needed between these two full thoughts.

    It was 1969, and Buzz Aldrin had just completed the first moonwalk.

The above example is correct. Adding a connector word like *and, so, but,* etc. also solves the problem.

- **Semicolons (;)**

    Semicolons function exactly like periods; they must have a full sentence on each side of them. The only difference is that the word after the semicolon is not capitalized.

- **Colons (:)**

    A colon is used before expanding upon the statement made in the first sentence. <u>A colon always comes after a complete sentence</u>, but the statement after a colon does not have to be a complete sentence (it can be, though). Let's see some examples:

    He was celebrating a great accomplishment: he won the belching contest.

Notice how we expand upon the first sentence after the colon. The colon basically says *'and that accomplishment is.'*

    There are several items in my lunchbox: an apple, a sandwich, chips, and milk.

Here the colon is saying *'and those items are...'* Colons commonly come before lists, although they do not come before every list...

    My favorite bands are: The Donkeys, Purple Jam, and The Sammy Schmoos.

<u>Above is an incorrect use of a colon.</u> First of all, the part before the colon is not a complete sentence. Secondly, a colon also is a stop in speech, and this sentence would sound smoother if we read it without a pause or stop after the word "are."

Note: If you are reading closely, you may say, "Wait a second Mr. Writer. You are misusing colons in this book!" If you are using an informal or outline style of writing (like this book does), it is OK to use colons to improve organization. However, you will never see this style of writing on the ACT English Test; stick to the rules above.

- **Dashes (–)**

    Most simply, a dash is an extended pause. In many ways dashes are similar to commas, and in other ways they are similar to colons. Basically, you use them anytime you are trying to pause and build a little tension before continuing on with a sentence.

    We slowly looked inside the dark tomb – then the zombies emerged.

The second half of the sentence gets some extra emphasis, as the dash builds tension.

    His car – a 1959 Corvette – was the fastest in town.

Just as with commas, dashes can surround extra information added to a sentence. Technically the dashes add extra emphasis to the surrounded statement, but ACT will never make you choose between double commas or double dashes. Just make sure you don't use one of each to surround the extra information. That is incorrect.

> She is a fan of many arts – opera, ballet, and especially tap dance.

In this sentence we could have used a colon. A dash can be used in any place a colon can be used. Finally, notice that dashes can go between complete sentences or within one sentence. As long as you have an occasion for a long, tension-building pause, a dash will work.

Note: Although a dash was grammatically OK in the previous sentence, a colon would have been better. Why? The tension-building effect of the dash is unnecessary given the content of the sentence.

- **Who vs. Whom**

    There is a simple trick to figuring out when to use *who* and when to use *whom*. *Who* is used in places where the words *he*, *she*, or *they* would fit. *Whom* is used in places where the words *him*, *her*, or *them* would fit. Let's see some example sentences to illustrate. All of the following examples are grammatically correct.

    > It is the goalie **who** plays the best.

'He plays the best' sounds better than 'him plays the best,' so *who* is better than *whom*.

> They were good friends **who** never argued, friends **who** always got along.

'They never argued' and 'they always got along' both sound good. *Who* is correct in both cases. Note that you ignore the beginning of the sentence when using this trick.

Using *whom* can be a little trickier, but it just takes some practice.

> The Smiths were relatives **whom** she had never met.

'They she had never met' sounds wrong; 'them she had never met' sounds wrong too. So which is correct? When using this trick with *whom* you often have to change the word order slightly. 'She had never met them' sounds good, so *whom* is correct.

Note: Search online for "who versus whom exercises" for more practice.

- **Working with Titles and Names**

    The blacksmith, John Anderson, made horseshoes for the town.

    The blacksmith John Anderson made horseshoes for the town.

Which is correct? Both. When a title (blacksmith, musician, writer, etc.) appears before a name, we can usually punctuate it either with commas surrounding the name or with no commas at all. This is not always true, though.

    The politician Ronald Reagan once said, "America is too great for small dreams."

    The politician, Ronald Reagan, once said, "America is too great for small dreams."

Which is correct? Only the first sentence. When the name is essential to the meaning of the sentence, it is not surrounded by commas. In the first example, the name "John Anderson" could be left out. Leaving out "Ronald Reagan" would be awkward.

Note: As usual, the correct option is also the one that sounds the best when read aloud.

- **Possession and Apostrophes**

    Apostrophe usage is easy with a little practice. Let's use some examples to see how apostrophes are applied. Then we will sum up the rules at the end.

    A) The team's field is painted for action.

    B) The teams are playing in an important game.

    C) The teams' cheerleaders are staring each other down.

The three examples above are all correct. We can confirm this by asking two simple questions about each sentence.

    1) Whose _____ is it? (to determine if there is possession)

    2) Was it plural already? (to determine where the apostrophe goes)

        Let's look back at sentences A, B, and C:

Sentence A — First we ask, "Whose field is it?" The answer is "It is the team's field." Now we know there is possession, and thus an apostrophe is needed. The next question is "Was it plural already?" No, we are talking about one team here, so the apostrophe goes before the s.

Sentence B — "Whose 'are playing' is it?" This just doesn't work. There is no possession, and therefore no apostrophe is needed.

Sentence C — "Whose cheerleaders are they?" The answer is "They are the teams' cheerleaders." So we have possession and need an apostrophe. "Was it plural already?" Yes, we are talking about two teams and their cheerleaders. Therefore, the apostrophe goes after the s. (This is assuming that cheerleaders from opposite teams are staring at each other, not that girls on the same squad are in a stare down! In that case it would be only one team's cheerleaders and the apostrophe would go before the s)

The lesson: If there is possession, an apostrophe is needed. If the thing that has possession is plural already, then the apostrophe comes after the s. If just one singular thing has possession, the apostrophe comes before the s.

Note: Apostrophes are easy to understand with a little practice. Search online for "apostrophe rules" or "apostrophe exercises" if you need a bit more help.

- **Defining Those You Describe**

    Again, this concept is best illustrated through examples:

    A) Driving towards the park, Joe saw a tiger.
    B) Driving towards the park, a tiger appeared.

Only the first sentence (A) is correct. When a sentence starts with a verb phrase like "driving towards the park," "jogging away from home," etc., we immediately need to define who is performing the action before continuing with the sentence. In example A, it is Joe who is driving, so we put his name right after the verb phrase. Even if the whole passage had focused on Joe driving, and we are certain that Joe is the person the sentence is talking about, example B would still be incorrect. The only way example B would work is if the tiger was driving!

   A) An amazing hitter, Willie Mays is my favorite baseball player.
   B) An amazing hitter, I truly enjoy Willie Mays.

Only the first sentence (A) is correct. When a sentence starts with a descriptive phrase like "an amazing hitter," "a great man," etc., we immediately need to define who that person is before continuing the sentence. So in example A, "Willie Mays" is written right after the opening phrase. Notice how example B almost sounds like "I" am the person who is the amazing hitter.

A) Heading into a dark field, snow began to fall onto the bus.
B) As the bus headed into a dark field, snow began to fall onto it.

Only the second sentence (B) is correct. Example A has the same problem we saw before: not immediately defining what is "heading into a dark field." Example A would only work if it was the snow that was heading into the field, not the bus. Example B is a bit different; it indicates that the bus is heading into the field in the first part of the sentence. Since we already know what is performing the action, we don't need to worry about defining it (writing "the bus") after the comma.

Note: Occasionally you will see a description come after a noun at the end of a sentence. For example, "I am a big fan of Willie Mays, a great baseball player" or "The band is playing at Smith Field, a 10,000 seat stadium." As long as the description and noun are right next to each other, these sentences are also grammatically OK.

- **Special Cases of Apostrophes – Its, it's, and its' / who's and whose**

    It's: This means *it is*, as in 'It's a nice day outside.'

    Its: This is the possessive form of it, as in 'The dog wagged its tail' or 'The city had its 100th birthday today.'

    Its':   This is not a grammatically correct word. It will never be the right answer.

    Who's: This means *who is*, as in 'Who's going with me to the movie?'

    Whose: This is the possessive form, as in 'Whose shirt is this?' or 'Whose toy did I step on?'

- **Parallelism**

    Different words or phrases in the same sentence should follow the same basic pattern. Usually parallel wording just sounds right, but sometimes it takes some thought.

    Parallel (correct):   The professor enjoys writing papers, reading books, and researching literature.
    Not parallel (incorrect): The professor enjoys writing papers, reading books, and to research literature.

    "To research" is in a different form and is not parallel with the –ing form verbs.

| Parallel: | She is fast, agile, and <u>graceful</u>. |
| Not parallel: | She is fast, agile, and <u>has grace</u>. |

"Graceful" is an adjective, just like "fast" and "agile." "Has grace" takes a different form than the other descriptors. Note that parallel sentences tend to flow better than nonparallel sentences.

| Parallel: | They enjoyed traveling to <u>the mountain</u> and <u>the beach</u>. |
| Not parallel: | They enjoyed traveling to <u>the mountain</u> and to <u>the sandy expanse of the beach</u>. |

Although both sentences are grammatically correct, the flow of the 'not parallel' sentence is disrupted by adding the description. ACT would prefer that you leave out the description, especially because it does not add any legitimate information to the sentence (we already know that a beach is a sandy expanse).

- **Then vs. Than and Effect vs. Affect**

"Than" is only used in comparisons, as in 'Candy tastes better than beans.' "Then" has a few meanings that basically involve the passing of time. Just remember, if it's a comparison, use "than." "Effect" is a noun, as in 'The effect of the storm is a power outage.' "Affect" is a verb, as in 'The defense affects his throw.'

- **Forms of "have" and "was" Changing Verbs**

Forms of "have" (have, has, and had) and "was" (was and were) change the past tense of certain irregular verbs. Let's see a few examples:

She <u>sang</u> the anthem.	She <u>has sung</u> for many years.
He <u>became</u> an author.	He <u>had</u> quickly <u>become</u> a skilled writer.
We <u>knew</u> the test was hard.	It <u>was known</u> that we failed.

There is a long list of verbs that change in a similar way. Generally you can get these questions correct by simply choosing the word that sounds right. However, if you are not sure what is correct, check to see if a form of "have" or "was" is changing the verb. An online search for "irregular verbs" will return many more examples of this rule.

Next Step: Now that you have made it through this chapter, try the English Test of ACT form 64E. After you complete the test, review the answers and explanations found on page 114 of this book (learn from your mistakes!). ACT form 64E can be downloaded at ACTPowerPrep.com.

Chapter 2 – Math

Read through this chapter, and then try a practice test. You can reference the formulas on pages 32 to 37 while taking practice tests – just make sure you memorize them before you take the real thing.

Format and Basic Strategy

The ACT Math Test covers a wide range of algebra and geometry concepts, as well as a small amount of trigonometry. You get 60 minutes to complete 60 questions, for an average of one question per minute. **Math Test questions start easy and get more difficult as the test goes on.** For example, #20 is harder than #1, #30 is harder than #20, and so on. Use your time wisely; if you find #40 – 60 to be extremely difficult, spend extra time on the earlier questions and make sure you get those correct. If you believe you can solve the more difficult questions, save time for them by getting through the easier questions quickly. Just watch out for 'stupid mistakes' and don't leave any questions blank. Practice and have your strategy set before going into the test.

This chapter contains more formulas, examples, and academic information than the others. Tips and tricks help a bit, but you need to know mathematical concepts to truly excel on this test. Still, don't worry if you have not learned every concept you see on the Math Test; just **master the concepts you have previously learned in math class. It takes many hours to learn entirely new mathematical ideas. It is relatively easy to relearn concepts from past math classes.**

This section begins with a listing of the mathematical concepts found on the test (pages 29 to 31). A list of the formulas commonly used on the ACT appears on pages 32 to 37. Next, pages 38 to 43 give some tips and tricks to help you through the test. Finally, pages 44 to 56 contain practice problems that mirror the most commonly asked Math Test questions.

In the tips and tricks section, I mark each example as a low or high difficulty question. If math is not a strength for you, don't worry if some questions look puzzling. The high difficulty questions are designed for students looking to score 27 or higher on the Math Test. The questions in the practice problems section (titled *30 Examples for the 30 Most Important Concepts*) are not given a difficulty. They simply start easy and get more difficult as they go, just as on a real ACT Math Test.

A Note on Calculators

Most calculators are allowed on the ACT Math Test. I recommend using a TI-83 Plus or TI-84 Plus calculator because they are user friendly, have a large display, and are capable of performing all the necessary mathematical functions. Most of the older TI models also work well, but some of the newer models are prohibited. Check the website below to see if your calculator is allowed.

No rules prohibit programming formulas and solvers into your calculator. At our website, Superior Test Preparation offers an inexpensive download of roughly 20 formulas and solvers that can be programmed into your calculator. The programs walk you through certain calculations that are common on the ACT. It is best to memorize the formulas, but if you think you may forget a few, the programs can be quite helpful.

The official list of calculator rules is found here:

www.actstudent.org/faq/answers/calculator.html

Further information on calculator programs can be found at the ACT Power Preparation site:

www.ACTPowerPrep.com

Listing of Math Concepts Found on the ACT Test

It would take hundreds of pages to fully explain every math concept found on the ACT, so instead I will give a list of the math skills necessary for the test. Search online or consult a math book if you need to refresh your skills in any of these areas. Also, many of these ideas are explained briefly in the practice problems section on pages 44 – 56 of this book. Whenever you study math, the key is to do as many problems as possible. Keep working on practice ACT Tests and always correct your work to learn from your mistakes!

Note: As mentioned in the introduction, the goal for the ACT is not to learn a bunch of new math concepts. Learning entirely new disciplines of math could take months! The goal is to master the concepts you have already learned in the past. If you don't know Trigonometry, don't worry about it. Trigonometry is a small part of the test anyway.

Pre-Algebra / Elementary Algebra – 24 of the 60 questions on each test are based on the following topics

- Basic addition, subtraction, multiplying, and dividing of integers, decimals, and fractions
- Order of operations (PEMDAS)
- Distributing terms in equations
- Basic math with square roots
- Basic math with exponents
- Scientific notation
- Factoring and simplifying fractions and equations
- Ratios, proportions, and percentages
- Basic logic problems
- The equation of a line
- Absolute values
- Working on a number line
- Simple probabilities
- Basic interpretation of tables and graphs
- Working with simple statistics (average or mean, median, mode, range)
- Mathematical substitution
- Factoring and solving quadratic equations
- FOIL and distribution

- Creating variables and basic equations from word problems
- Basic combinations

Intermediate Algebra – 9 questions per test are based on the following topics

- The quadratic formula
- Rational expressions (fractions with polynomials in them)
- Radical expressions (more advanced work with square roots – using them in equations, simplifying, etc.)
- Equations and inequalities involving absolute values
- Algebraic and geometric sequences; mathematical patterns
- Systems of equations
- Complex numbers (imaginary numbers)
- Functions – $f(x)$, $g(x)$, $f(g(x))$, etc.
- Solving polynomial equations
- Creating variables and equations from word problems using more advanced algebra
- Basic logarithms

Coordinate Geometry – 9 questions per test are based on the following topics

- Graphing equations, points, lines, etc.
- Making conclusions from graphs
- Basic facts about polynomial and circle graphs (and occasionally other conic graphs)
- Distance, midpoint, and slope
- Working with parallel and perpendicular lines

Plane Geometry – 14 questions per test are based on the following topics

- Angle measurements in shapes, parallel lines, and perpendicular lines (all the basic angle rules from geometric proofs)
- Area, perimeter, and facts about angles for the following shapes: circles, triangles, rectangles, parallelograms, and trapezoids
- Volume and surface area for 3 dimensional figures (usually just geometric prisms)
- Reflecting and rotating graphs and figures
- Working with shapes in two and three dimensions (usually involving logic, basic algebra, and/ or basic geometry)

Trigonometry – 4 questions per test are based on the following topics

- SOHCAHTOA (1 – 3 of the trigonometry questions are always based on SOHCAHTOA)
- Graphing trig functions
- Solving trig-related equations
- Basic trig identities
- Law of sines and law of cosines
- Converting radians to degrees

Note: This list covers about 95% of what you will see on test day, but sometimes ACT does throw you a random math topic out of the blue. The topic will always be based off algebra, geometry, or introductory trigonometry.

Note: Although the questions are based off of these concepts, ACT often finds unusual ways to present the material. There are not many 'normal-looking' equations on the ACT. Practice and you will become familiar with this.

ACT Math Formula Sheet

Extra space is left on each page to add notes, examples, additional concepts, etc.

Triangles

Area = ½(base x height)

The 3 angles add to 180⁰

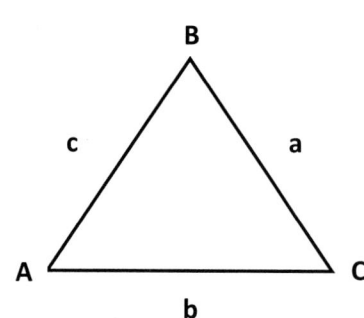

Right Triangles: (contain a 90⁰ angle)
The formulas above apply here as well
Pythagorean Theorem: $a^2 + b^2 = c^2$

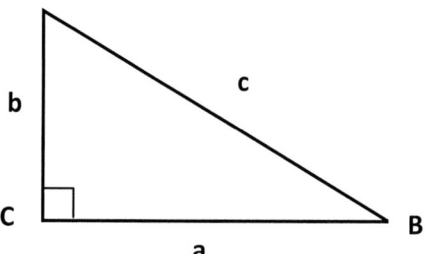

Equilateral Triangle – All sides are the same length, all angles are 60⁰.
Isosceles Triangle – Two sides are the same length; the angles opposite these two sides are the same.

Similar Triangles – Two different triangles with the same angle measures; their side lengths and perimeters will be proportional.
Example: All sides on the second triangle are ½ the length of the sides on the first triangle.
Notice how all angle measures are identical. *(figures are not to scale)*

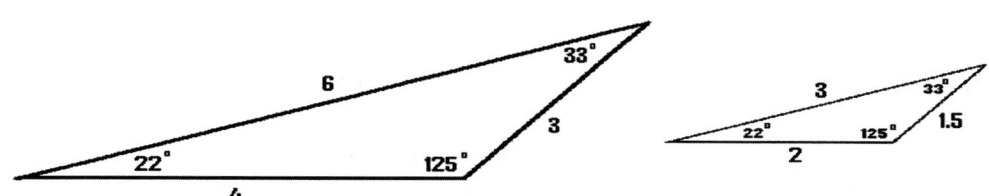

SOH CAH TOA – a law of any right triangle

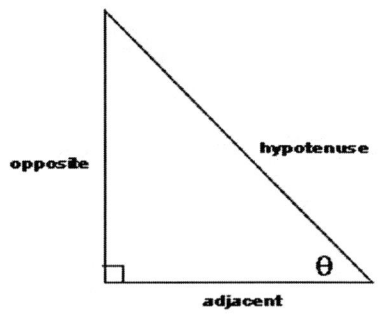

SOH $\sin \theta =$ Opposite ÷ Hypotenuse
CAH $\cos \theta =$ Adjacent ÷ Hypotenuse
TOA $\tan \theta =$ Opposite ÷ Adjacent

Circles

Equation of a circle = $(x-h)^2 + (y-k)^2 = r^2$
r is the radius, h and k are the x and y points of the center respectively
Example: $(x-4)^2 + (y+3)^2 = 100$
This would be a circle centered at (4,-3) with a radius of 10

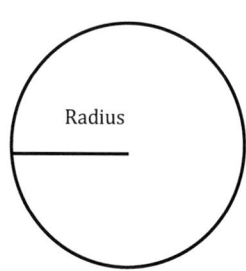

Area of a circle = πr^2 Full circle = 360°   Circumference of a circle = $2\pi r$

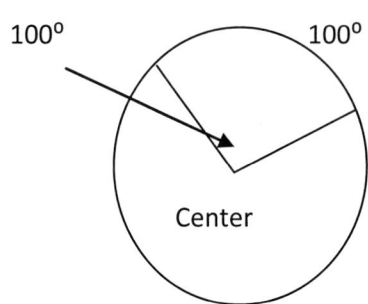

The measure of the arc is the same as the measure of the interior angle made from the center point.

Other Geometric Shapes

> Diagrams on the ACT Math Test are pretty accurate. If lines, diagonals, angles, etc. look to have the same measure, chances are that they do.

Squares

Area = S x S

Perimeter = 4S

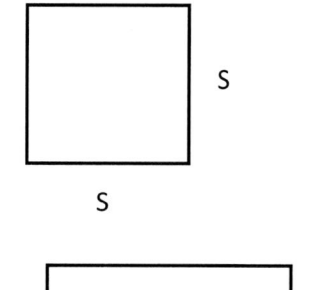

Rectangles

Area = L x W

Perimeter = 2L + 2W

Parallelogram

Area = base x height

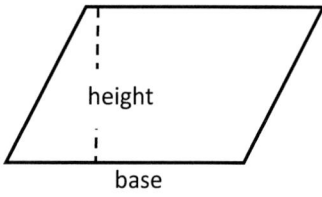

A *Rhombus* is a parallelogram with four equal sides. Its diagonals meet at right angles and bisect each other.

Trapezoid

Area = ½(base1 +base2) x height

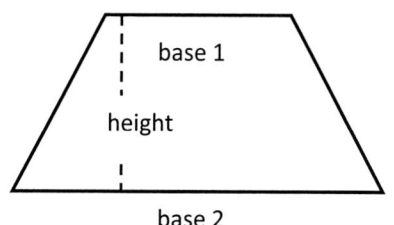

An *Isosceles Trapezoid* has two equal sides. Its diagonals divide each other into equal segments.

Geometric Prism (a 3-D box)

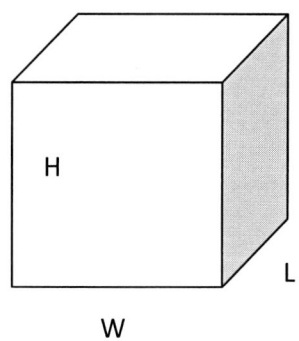

Volume = length x width x height

Surface Area = 2LW + 2LH + 2HW

(Surface Area = the flat areas of all six sides of the box added up)

A *cube* is a geometric prism in which the length, width, and height are all the same.

Angle Measures

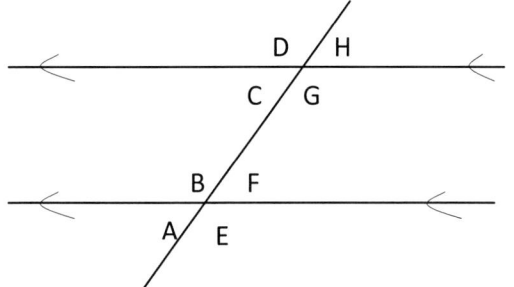

When a line crosses two parallel lines several rules apply:
- Corresponding angles are congruent:
$\angle A = \angle C \quad \angle B = \angle D \quad \angle E = \angle G \quad \angle F = \angle H$
- Alternate exterior angles are congruent; alternate interior angles are congruent:
$\angle A = \angle H \quad \angle B = \angle G \quad \angle E = \angle D \quad \angle F = \angle C$
- Straight lines add to 180°:
$\angle A + \angle B = 180° \quad \angle G + C = 180° \ ...$ Etc.
- For any lines that cross, the angles across from each other are congruent, a concept called "vertical angles":
$\angle A = \angle F \quad \angle B = \angle E \quad \angle C = \angle H \quad \angle D = \angle G$

Basically, all the angles that look the same, are the same!

Lines

Slope Intercept Form: y = mx + b

where x and y represent a point on the line, m is the slope, and b is the y intercept

Slope = $\frac{y_2 - y_1}{x_2 - x_1}$

Parallel lines have the same slope.

Perpendicular lines have negative reciprocal slopes.

Example: Line A slope = 3/5, the perpendicular Line B would have a slope of -5/3

Distance = $\sqrt{(x_2 - x_1)^2 + (y_2 - y_1)^2}$

Example: Find the distance between (4,9) and (8,6)

$\sqrt{(8-4)^2 + (6-9)^2} \ = \ \sqrt{25} \ = \ 5$

Midpoint = $(\frac{x_1 + x_2}{2}, \frac{y_1 + y_2}{2})$

Example: Find the midpoint between (6,5) and (10,-1)

$(\frac{6+10}{2}, \frac{5+(-1)}{2}) \ = \ (8,2)$

Sequences and Combinations

Arithmetic Sequences – sequences by addition or subtraction. Example: 2, 4, 6, 8 or 18, 10, 2, -6

Geometric Sequences – sequences by multiplication or division. Example: 3, 9, 27 or 100, 50, 25

Basic Combinations – You have 5 shirts, 8 pairs of pants, and 3 hats. How many different outfits of 1 shirt, 1 pair of pants, and 1 hat do you have?

5 x 8 x 3 = 120 combinations – *you just multiply the number of options for each component*

Advanced Algebra and Definitions

$X^3(X^2) = X^5$	$(X^3)^3 = X^9$	$2X^3 + X^3 = 3X^3$	$4X^6(8X^2) = 32X^8$
Add the exponents	Multiply the exponents	Combine like terms	Multiply terms, add exponents

Function problems involving f(x), g(x), etc. require basic substitution.

Example: $F(x) = x^2 + 3$ $\quad F(2) = 2^2 + 3 = 7 \quad$ $F(x+h) = (x+h)^2 + 3$

Distance = Rate x Time

Example: 3 hours at 70 mph = 70 x 3 = 210 miles traveled

Integers:	Numbers without fractions or decimals (….-4,-3,-2,-1, 0, 1, 2, 3, 4….)
Rational Numbers:	Any integer, fraction, terminating decimal, or repeating decimal. The opposite are <u>Irrational Numbers</u>. Irrational numbers have decimals that neither terminate (end) nor repeat; they go on forever with no pattern. Square roots and π are the only irrational numbers seen on the ACT.
Real Numbers:	All rational and irrational numbers. Numbers involving *i* and negative square roots are the only 'not real' or 'imaginary' numbers.
Prime Numbers:	Numbers that can only be divided evenly by 1 and themselves. Examples: 2, 5, 7, 13, 29, 41

Further Reading for those Looking to Score Above 30

A few more advanced concepts occasionally appear near the end of the test. I will not give these formulas due to their complexity and because they only make up a very small portion of the test (about 2 – 5 questions total). Search for the following concepts online or in a math book if you are interested in learning them. You do not have to know them in depth; the basics will do.

Triangles:	the law of sines and the law of cosines
Imaginary Numbers:	the equivalents of i, i^2, i^3, and i^4; working with i in algebra problems
Logarithms:	the basic identities of a logarithm
Trigonometric Graphs:	defining the period and amplitude; knowing the basic shape of sine and cosine graphs
Trig Functions:	which function(s) are positive and negative in each quadrant (the *All Students Take Calculus* trick); finding inverses on a calculator ($\sin^{-1}, \cos^{-1}, \tan^{-1}$); using SOHCAHTOA within a coordinate plane; converting radians to degrees.

Note: *These formulas are easier than they sound, but they are not all that important. I don't recommend learning a formula unless you have previously worked with it in a math class.*

Math Tips, Tricks, and Strategies

1. ***Your Calculator is Your Friend***

    The calculator is a powerful tool for the ACT Math Test. In addition to its use for basic mathematical functions, it can solve difficult problems more quickly than through complicated formulas. Perhaps most importantly, it can be used to figure out problems you otherwise may not know. Here are two examples:

    Bill has decided to get in shape for the upcoming football season. He decided to do 25 sit ups today (day 1) and 10 additional each day for the next month. How many sit ups will Bill do over the 30 day month? **Difficulty: Low**

    A. 4160
    B. 4750
    C. 5100
    D. 5350
    E. 7325

The correct answer is C. I immediately start punching numbers in my calculator when I see a problem like this one (25 + 35 + 45...). As long as you can keep count of how many numbers you have punched in, you can easily finish a problem like this in a minute or two. Time yourself and I bet you are surprised how fast your calculator can perform long problems such as this one.

Note: The formula for the sum of an arithmetic sequence could also be used to complete this problem. This formula is not included on the formula sheet because of its complexity (and your calculator can do the job anyway).

Here is a more advanced example of using your calculator to solve a problem you otherwise might not know:

For $0° < x < 360°$, if $\sin x < 0$ and $\cos x > 0$, what are the possible values of x?
Difficulty: High

A. x = 180° or 360°
B. $0 < x < 90°$
C. $90° < x < 180°$
D. $180° < x < 270°$
E. $270° < x < 360°$

The correct answer is E. Here's one way to solve this problem with your TI calculator:

Step 1 – Press 'Mode' then choose 'Degree' (ACT rarely asks questions using radian measures. Keep your calculator in degree mode at all times.)

Step 2 – Begin to test values. So if you are testing answer B, you will find the sin and cos of a value between 0° and 90°. For this walkthrough, let's use 45° as the test value.

Enter sin(45) into your calculator. You will find that it equals .71. Choice B would now be disqualified because the sin is positive (the directions say sin must be < 0). Following this testing process for each answer choice, you will soon find that only a value between 270° and 360° returns a negative sin and positive cos, which is what the problem asks for.

Note: The 'All Students Take Calculus' trick would be the easiest way to solve the preceding problem. Search online for "All Students Take Calculus" if you are interested in learning it. It's quite simple and it will help on ACT questions like this one.

Note: Different problems present different ways to utilize your calculator. Be creative; graphing calculators are powerful tools.

2. ***Find a Formula that Works***

   Most questions, even the hardest ones, will fit into a basic mathematical formula or method (most of which are covered in this book). ACT will not surprise you with a question about Calculus. As the test goes on and the questions get more difficult, the concepts still remain fairly similar. Although more advanced math concepts do appear occasionally, the harder questions often require the same algebra and geometry knowledge you used for the easier problems. What is getting harder is the logic to find the right methods to solve the problem. So don't assume a question is too difficult for you; **think 'What formula(s) could apply here?' or 'How could I get the information I need?'** and you may be led to the solution. Here is an extended example:

   A 5 inch by 12 inch rectangle is inscribed in a circle as shown below. Which is closest to the area of the circle in square inches?   **Difficulty: High**

   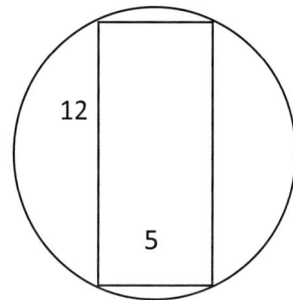

   A. 12π
   B. 34π
   C. 42π
   D. 63π
   E. 165π

The correct answer is C. This problem seems difficult, but it can be solved with relatively simple mathematical ideas. **First, think about what information you will need. In this case, you want the area of the circle (Area = πr²), so you will need to find the radius.** Next, check out the information given to you. The Math Test usually does not give much unnecessary information, so chances are you will need to work with the given rectangle. Now the one tricky part – by drawing a diagonal on the rectangle you form a diameter, which is equal to twice the radius (see figure below).

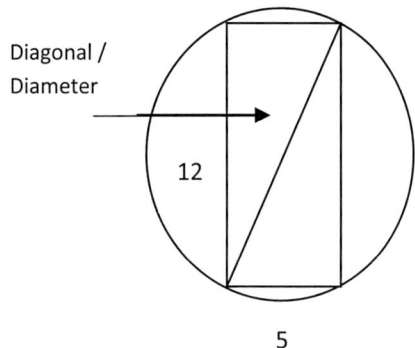

Since adding the diagonal created a right triangle, we can find the length of the diameter with the Pythagorean Theorem:

$a^2 + b^2 = c^2$

$5^2 + 12^2 = diameter^2$

$diameter^2 = 169$, $diameter = 13$

$radius = .5(13) = 6.5$

$area = \pi r^2 = \pi 6.5^2 = 42.25\pi$

We just completed a very difficult ACT problem using only the Pythagorean Theorem and the area of a circle formula. Find the formula that makes sense for the situation; chances are the math is easier than it looks.

Note: *This problem provides a great example of another trick. Say this problem just plain stumped you. You still want to make an educated guess using any information you know.*

Maybe you remember the area of a rectangle formula, area = length x width. So, the area of the rectangle equals 60. In my opinion, the circle looks about twice as big as the rectangle. So I will guess the area of the circle is about 2 x 60 = 120 square inches. Next, I test the answers and see which numbers are near my educated guess. Choice C gives us 42 x π, which equals 131.95 – pretty close to my guess of 120. This answer seems to make sense. Choice B, which equals 106.81, would be a fair option as well. The other choices are way too high or low and should not be considered. **The main point – if possible, use logic and your calculator to narrow down choices and make a more accurate guess.**

3. *Use Dummy Numbers to make Problems Easier*

Most students agree that it is easier to work with actual numbers than with variables. By using 'dummy numbers' you can turn a problem involving variables into one with regular numbers. You can use dummy numbers on most problems involving simplification, on any problem that says something like "if X is any integer...", and in a few other assorted situations. I will illustrate dummy numbers through a simple example. Then we will try a more difficult application of dummies (dummy numbers are usually most helpful on difficult problems).

The expression $4(x + 9) - 2(3x - 6)$ equals: **Difficulty: Low**

A. $-x + 24$
B. $x + 30$
C. $-2x + 30$
D. $-2x + 40$
E. $-2x + 48$

The correct answer is E. This problem is fairly easy to complete algebraically, but it will also serve as a basic example of using 'dummies.' Using dummies is quite easy. You simply make x any number, complete the problem, and find which answer matches up. You want to use a small number for ease, but avoid using 1 as your dummy.

So I'll say x=2. Now the given equation = $4(2 + 9) - 2(3(2) - 6) = 44$.
Next, I carry the dummy to the answers. Substituting x=2 in each answer choice shows that when x=2, choice E also equals 44 ($-2(2) + 48 = 44$). None of the other choices equal 44. Choice E is the only option that can be correct.

Note: Occasionally your dummy will return more than one answer choice that works. For example, say two options equaled 44 in the last example. When this happens, try a new dummy number (x=5, x=-2, etc.) in each choice that worked the first time; only one of the options will work every time.

If a and b are any positive integers, what value(s) of x, if any, will make $|ax - b| = |bx - a|$? **Difficulty: High**

A. $1, -1$
B. 2
C. $\frac{a+b}{a-b}$
D. all real integers
E. no real integers

The correct answer is A. First of all, you must know how to work with *absolute values* to complete this problem (if you don't know the concept, look it up). Now we will use dummy numbers to make this problem much easier:

a and b can both be any positive integer, so let's use a = 2 and b = 3 (those certainly fit the description of "any positive integers"). Now the problem looks like this:

$|2x - 3| = |3x - 2|$

It is difficult to do algebra when two absolute values are involved, so we will work backwards and see which answer fits.

Choice A: x = 1 $|2(1) - 3| = |3(1) - 2|$ True ; x = -1 $|2(-1) - 3| = |3(-1) - 2|$ True

Thus, choice A works. At this point you could eliminate every other option except for D. -1 and 1 are real integers, so choice D could still possibly be correct. Now let's test a new x value to see if D is correct.

x=5 $|2(5) - 3| = |3(5) - 2|$ False

Since x=5 does not make this expression true, "all real integers" cannot be the value of x, and A is confirmed as the right answer.

Note: You will get the same results whether you use a = 2 and b = 3 or you use a = 8 and b = 35. The directions said only that a and b are positive integers, so any positive numbers will work.

4. **Draw! Plot! Test! Write the Info and Find an X!**

   Struggling with a problem? Try one of these tactics to get going in the right direction:

   a. *Draw*

      Here's a tip you have heard from math teachers for years. Draw diagrams whenever you can. It always helps to visualize a problem, especially when working with word problems.

      *Note: On many problems ACT will provide you with a diagram. While the directions say that these drawings are not to scale, they usually are very close. For example, **if two sides of a shape look the same, they probably are the same.***

   b. *Plot*

      For problems involving equations of lines or X and Y axis graphs, manually plotting lines and/or points can help to clarify the problem or at least narrow down the possibilities. Additionally, you can use the 'Y=' button on your graphing calculator to plot more complex graphs.

c. *Test*

Test answer choices to see if they fit in the problem ('working backwards'). Eliminate answer choices that do not seem to make sense. Be creative; different problems present different ways to test values. **Sometimes working backwards is faster and more accurate than doing a problem the conventional way.**

Note: When working backwards, it is usually best to try choice C first. Choice C will be the middle number, and you can often figure out if your answer will be higher or lower than that number. This will narrow down your choices quickly.

d. *Write the Info and Find an X*

Start the problem by writing out all the mathematical information you are given. Then establish exactly what you are looking for; this will be your 'X' variable (or Y or Z or whatever you want to call it). Now try to find a bridge from the information you are given to the value of your 'X' variable. The bridge will be some kind of formula or math concept.

Next Step: First, proceed to the next section, which gives examples of the most common math questions on the ACT Test. After that, try the Math Test from ACT form 64E. A link to the form is available at ACTPowerPrep.com. After completing that test, correct it with the answers and explanations found on page 121 of this book.

The best way to improve on the ACT Math Test is to complete practice problems, correct them, and learn from your mistakes. If you have forgotten how to do a particular problem, look it up online or ask your math teacher for help.

30 Examples for the 30 Most Important Concepts

Try to solve each problem as you go through this section (cover the answer with a piece of paper). Questions get harder as the section progresses. Short explanations are given, but further information on all of these concepts can easily be found online or in a math book.

Note: Since the goal is to master the math concepts behind these problems, most do not give answer choices.

1) Simplify: $2(x-4) - 7(x+2)$

Distribute first: $\quad 2x - 8 - 7x - 14$

Then combine like terms to get the answer: $\quad -5x - 22$

2) A point (-4,6) in a standard (x,y) plane is moved left 3 units and down 9 units. What are the new coordinates of the point?

The safest way to solve this question is by drawing a coordinate plane and visualizing the movement.

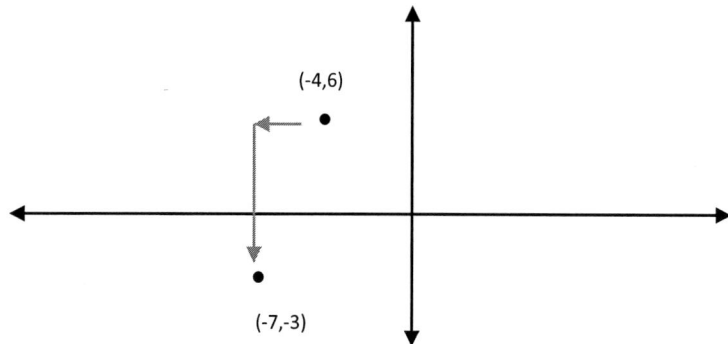

Moving 3 left brings the x coordinate to -7   *Moving 9 down brings the y coordinate to -3*

3) At the bowling alley's annual party, league members pay $15 for the dinner, while nonmembers pay $19 for the dinner. What is the total amount of money the alley makes from selling 60 tickets to league members and *p* tickets to nonmembers? (see options)

a) 19(p+60)   b) 19(p+15)   c) 15(60)+19p   d) p+60   e)(15+19)p

The correct answer is C. The 60 members pay $15 each, and the p nonmembers pay $19 each, so the total amount of money equals: $\quad 60 \text{ people} \times \$15 + p \text{ people} \times \$19$

4) What is the perimeter and area of a rectangle with a length of 9 in. and a width of 5 in.?

For perimeter simply add up all of the outer sides: $9 + 9 + 5 + 5 = 28$ *inches*

Area = Length × Width *Area* $= 9 \times 5 = 45$ *square inches*

It can be helpful to draw a picture on any problem like this one.

5) The number, N, of ants that will be in the ant farm through week *p* is modeled by the function $N(p) = \frac{700p^2 + 90}{p^2 + 2}$. Based on this model, roughly how many ants will be in the farm by week 3?

Number of ants through week 3: $N(3) = \dfrac{700(3^2) + 90}{3^2 + 2} = \dfrac{700(9) + 90}{9 + 2} \approx 581$ *ants*

6) Sketch a graph of this line below: $y = \frac{2}{3}x - 2$.

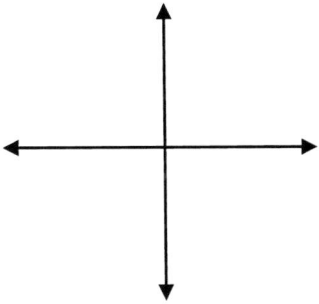

Correct answer:

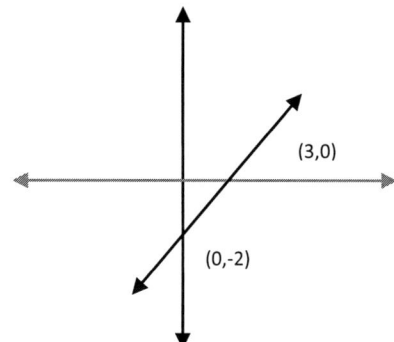

Being able to graph lines is important for the ACT. The easiest way is to find the Y intercept first – the Y intercept is always "b" in the form y=mx+b. Let's prove that for this example:

$$y = \frac{2}{3}(0) - 2 \qquad \text{when } x \text{ equals } 0, y \text{ equals } -2 \text{ so } (0, -2) \text{ is a point on the graph.}$$

Next, continue to find points (put in a number for x, find the y), and then connect the dots.

Another option: in y=mx+b, m is the slope. Since the slope is $\frac{2}{3}$, we can go up 2 and to the right 3 to find the next point (we still need to find the Y intercept to start from).

7) Solve: $|3 - 2| - |4 - 6|$

With absolute values, you simply must complete the math inside the brackets, and then turn any negative number positive. Positive numbers do not change.

$|3 - 2| = |1| = 1$ $\qquad\qquad$ $|4 - 6| = |-2| = 2$ $\qquad\qquad$ **$1 - 2 = -1$**

8) Find missing angles ACB and BCD. Points A, C, and D are collinear (on the same line).

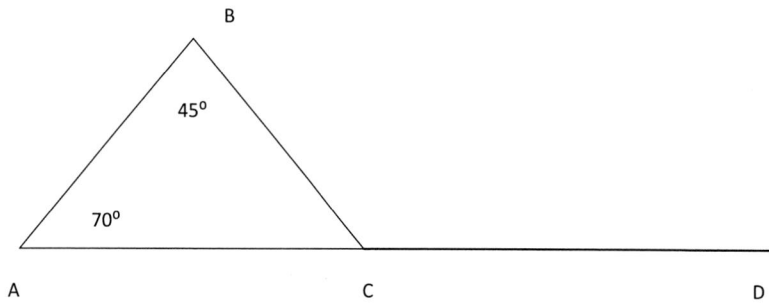

Angle ACB measures 65° because all triangles must add to 180°.   (180 - 70 - 45 = 65)

Angle BCD measures 115° because all straight lines must add to 180°. (180 - 65 = 115)

9) Simplify the following expressions (make each into one single fraction):

a) $\frac{8x}{5} - \frac{2y}{3}$ $\qquad\qquad$ b) $\frac{8x}{5} \times \frac{2y}{3}$ $\qquad\qquad$ c) $\frac{8x}{5} \div \frac{2y}{3}$

a) Get a common denominator, and then subtract:

$\frac{8x}{5}\left(\frac{3}{3}\right) = \frac{24x}{15}$ $\qquad\qquad$ $\frac{2y}{3}\left(\frac{5}{5}\right) = \frac{10y}{15}$ $\qquad\qquad$ $\frac{24x}{15} - \frac{10y}{15} = \frac{24x - 10y}{15}$

b) Multiply across the tops and bottoms (no common denominator is needed for multiplication):

$$\frac{8x}{5} \times \frac{2y}{3} = \frac{16xy}{15}$$

c) To divide, flip the second fraction and then multiply across:

$$\frac{8x}{5} \div \frac{2y}{3} = \frac{8x}{5} \times \frac{3}{2y} = \frac{24x}{10y}$$

That fraction can then be reduced by taking out common factors:

$$\frac{24x \div 2}{10y \div 2} = \frac{12x}{5y}$$

10) Bill remembers that 15 miles per hour is equal to 22 feet per second. If Bill is going 65 miles per hour, what is his speed in feet per second?

This is a classic ratio problem. Just make sure the same labels are across from each other (miles per hour shouldn't be across from feet per second in the ratio).

$$\frac{15 \; miles \; per \; hour}{22 \; feet \; per \; second} = \frac{65 \; miles \; per \; hour}{x \; feet \; per \; second}$$

Cross multiply to get: $15(x) = 65(22)$ $x = {1430}/{15} = 95.33 \; feet \; per \; second$

11) Suzy went shopping at a sports store that was having a sale in which every item was 15% off at the register, including already discounted items. Suzy purchased a softball glove with an original price of $60 marked with a discount of 20% off of its original price. Suzy also had to pay 8% sales tax on the final price of the item. How much did Suzy pay for the glove?

Original price: $60

First discount: 20% off $= \$60 \times .20 = \$12 \; discount$ *New price:* $\$60 - \$12 = \$48$

Next discount: 15% off $= \$48 \times .15 = \$7.20 \; discount$ *New price:* $\$48 - \$7.20 = \$40.80$

Tax: 8% additional $= \$40.80 \times .08 = \$3.26 \; tax$ *New price:* $\$40.80 + \$3.26 = \$44.06$

Suzy paid $44.06 for the softball glove.

Note: You cannot combine the discounts and/or tax; it is essential to do these problems step-by-step. Also, make sure you write 8% as .08, not .8 (80% would be written as .8).

12) Simplify the following equations: a) $6x^3 \times 4x^5$ b) $(3x^4)^3$ c) $2x^2 + 5x + 7x^2 + 3$

a) *multiply numbers, add exponents:* $6x^3 \times 4x^5 = 24x^8$

b) *take number to the exponent, multiply exponents:* $(3x^4)^3 = (3)^3 x^{12} = 27x^{12}$

c) *only add terms with same exponents:* $2x^2 + 5x + 7x^2 + 3 = 9x^2 + 5x + 3$

13) The points (6,3) and (2,-7) lie on a coordinate plane. Find (a) the midpoint, (b) the distance, and (c) the slope between these points.

a) $Midpoint = (\frac{x_1 + x_2}{2}, \frac{y_1 + y_2}{2}) = (\frac{6+2}{2}, \frac{3-7}{2}) = (4, -2)$

b) $Distance = \sqrt{(x_2 - x_1)^2 + (y_2 - y_1)^2} = \sqrt{(2-6)^2 + (-7-3)^2} = \sqrt{16 + 100} = \sqrt{116}$

c) $Slope = \frac{y_2 - y_1}{x_2 - x_1} = \frac{-7-3}{2-6} = \frac{-10}{-4} = \frac{5}{2}$

14) The vertices of the trapezoid below have their (x,y) coordinates labeled. What is the area, in square units, of the trapezoid?

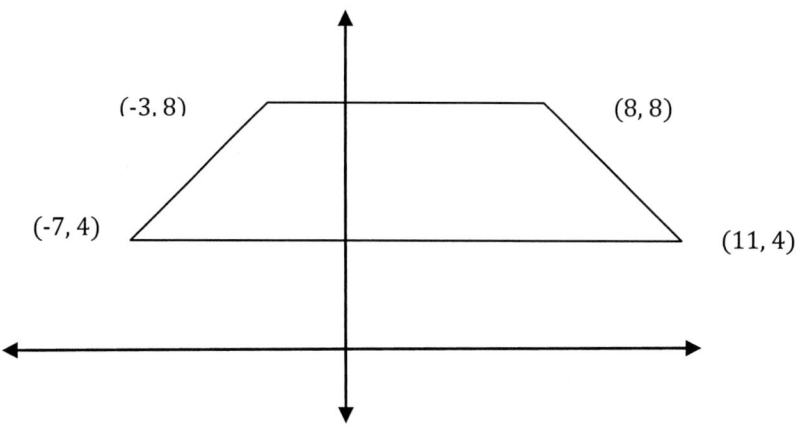

$$Area\ of\ a\ Trapezoid = \frac{1}{2}(base_1 + base_2)(height)$$

You could use the distance formula to find the length of the bases and the height, but it is not necessary. The length of a flat line is just the distance as if you were moving across a number line.

Length of bottom base $= 18$ (*straight across from* -7 *to* 11)

Length of top base $= 11$ (-3 *to* 8)

Height $= 4$ (*The bottom line is at* $y = 4$, *the top is at* $y = 8$)

$Area = \frac{1}{2}(18 + 11)(4) = 58$

15) In the figure below, all line segments intersect at right angles. Some side lengths are given. What is the area of the figure?

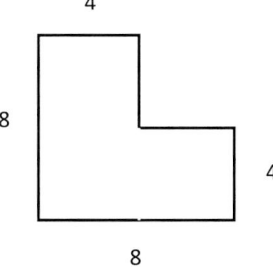

You are not expected to know a formula for the area of an L-shaped figure, so let's divide this into rectangles (think creatively!). We can also fill in the two remaining side lengths.

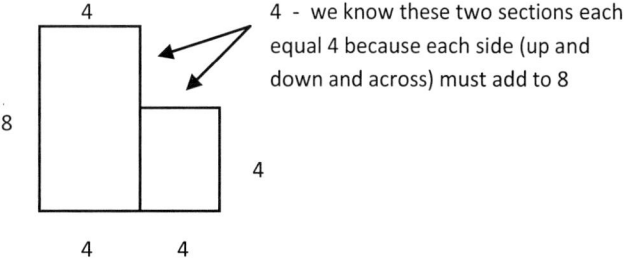

4 - we know these two sections each equal 4 because each side (up and down and across) must add to 8

$$Area\ left\ rect. = l \times w = 8 \times 4 = 32 \qquad Area\ right\ rect. = 4 \times 4 = 16$$

$$Total\ Area = 32 + 16 = 48$$

16) $f(x) = 2x - 3 \qquad g(x) = x^2 \qquad$ Find the following:

  a) $f(2) \qquad$ b) $g(-3) \qquad$ c) $f(g(4)) \qquad$ d) $f(g(x)) \qquad$ e) $g(f(x))$

These problems require working from the inside out. Substitute the number or function inside the parenthesis for the x in the outside function. Check out the explanations below.

a) $f(2) = 2(2) - 3 = 1 \qquad\qquad\qquad$ b) $g(-3) = (-3)^2 = 9$

For c) we still work from the inside out, we just add one more step.

c) $f(g(4)) = \quad$ step one: $\quad g(4) = 4^2 = 16 \quad$ step two: $\quad f(16) = 2(16) - 3 = 29$

For d) and e) we don't have a number in the parenthesis, so we have to substitute the entire equation for x instead.

d) $f(g(x)) = 2(x^2) - 3 \qquad\qquad\qquad$ e) $g(f(x)) = (2x - 3)^2$

17) Simplify the following fraction: $\dfrac{x^2+3x-10}{x^2-4}$

The top of the fraction (the numerator) can be factored into: $(x+5)(x-2)$

The bottom (denominator) is a perfect square that can be factored into: $(x+2)(x-2)$

The fraction now looks like this: $\dfrac{(x+5)(x-2)}{(x+2)(x-2)}$ *In this situation, the (x−2)'s on top and bottom will cancel each other out.*

The new, simplified fraction looks like this: $\dfrac{(x+5)}{(x+2)}$ *Nothing else can be cancelled out.*

18) What is a boat's average speed, in miles per hour, if it goes 75 miles in $2\frac{1}{2}$ hours?

$$Distance = Rate \times Time$$

Distance = 75 miles   *Rate (or speed) = x*   *Time = 2.5 hours*

75 miles = x(2.5 hours) $x = {75\ miles}/{2.5\ hours}$ *x = 30 miles per hour*

19) There are two triangles, Triangle A and Triangle B, drawn on a piece of paper. Triangle B has 4 times more height and a 3 times bigger base than Triangle A. How many times bigger is Triangle B's area than Triangle A's area?

$$Area\ of\ a\ Triangle = \frac{1}{2}(base)(height)$$

To make this easier, let's make up 'dummy numbers' (page 40) and actually compute the results.

Triangle A: Height = 2   Base = 3   (small, simple numbers usually are the best dummies)

Triangle B: Height = 8 (4× bigger than A, just as the directions said)   Base = 9 (3× bigger)

Area Triangle A=$\frac{1}{2}$(2)(3) = 3   *Area Triangle B=$\frac{1}{2}$(8)(9) = 36*

Triangle B's area is 12 times bigger than Triangle A's area.

20) Solve for the length of line JK in the following right triangle. The length of line JL is 20, and angle L is 55°. Angle K is 90°.

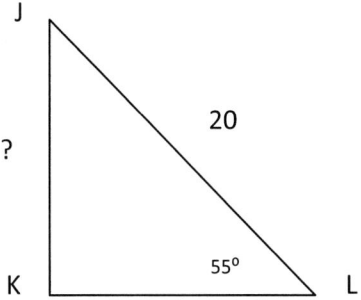

This is a classic SOHCAHTOA problem. We are given the value of line JL (which is the hypotenuse) and we want to find the measure of line JK (which is opposite the given angle). Thus, we will use Sin, which is equal to opposite divided by hypotenuse.

$$Sin\ 55° = {Line\ JK}/{20} \qquad Line\ JK = Sin\ 55° \times 20$$

If a numerical value is needed, we can type Sin 55 into the calculator.

$$Line\ JK = Sin\ 55° \times 20 \qquad .819 \times 20 = 16.3$$

Note: Anytime you are given one side and one angle of a right triangle, and the question asks for the length of another side, it is a SOHCAHTOA problem.

21) An engineer is given the measurements of a rectangular prism in terms of variables. The length is listed as (x-4), the width is listed as (x+1), and the height is listed as (2x+3). The engineer must turn these values into one polynomial equation for the volume of the prism. What is this equation?

$$Volume\ of\ a\ Rectangular\ Prism = Length \times Width \times Height$$

$Volume = (x - 4)(x + 1)(2x + 3)$ $\qquad$ *FOIL to get:* $(x^2 - 3x - 4)(2x + 3)$

Multiply the polynomials to get: $\quad 2x^3 + 3x^2 - 6x^2 - 9x - 8x - 12$

Combine like terms for the final answer: $\quad Volume = \quad 2x^3 - 3x^2 - 17x - 12$

22) A circle in a standard (x,y) coordinate plane has the equation $x^2 + (y - 4)^2 = 25$. What are the coordinates of the center of the circle and what is the length of the radius?

This question simply requires knowing the basics about the equation of a circle.

Center coordinates = (0,4) *notice how these fit in the equation to make the x and y expressions each equal zero:* $0^2 + (4-4)^2$

Radius = $\sqrt{25}$ = 5   *the radius is the square root of the number on the right side of the equation*

23) Bill drove his go-cart in a straight line at a constant speed. His friend recorded the distance, C feet, that Bill was from a certain tree at each second from t=0 to t=4 seconds. Bill put the results in the following table.

T	0	1	2	3	4
C	9	15	21	27	33

Which of the following five equations could represent the data above?

a) C=6t+9   b) C=t+9   c) C=9t+6   d) C=3t+3   e) C=15t

The correct answer is A, C=6t+9. If this equation is going to represent the data, the data must fit back into the equation. To clarify, let's plug the points in the table back into the equation:

t=0, C=9   9=6(0)+9 is true ;   t=1, C=15   15=6(1)+9 is true ;   t=2 C=21...

If you don't understand, try plugging the data points back into the incorrect choices. While some points may fit, you will always run into an incorrect equation eventually. For example, try the point t=2 seconds, C=21 feet – nothing works except C=6t+9.

24) Joe bought 60 sandwiches for the summer camp. Some of the sandwiches were Italian style, and the others were turkey. The Italian sandwiches cost $3.50, and the turkey sandwiches cost $2.70. Joe spent $190 on the sandwiches. How many turkey sandwiches did he buy?

We will start with a full mathematical explanation, and then we'll go through another approach.

We have two variables: $x =$ *the number of Italian sandwiches bought*
                          $y =$ *the number of turkey sandwiches bought*

First equation: there are 60 total sandwiches bought, so: $x + y = 60$

Second equation: we know the total cost of the sandwiches is $190, so:

$\$3.50(x) + \$2.70(y) = \$190$ that is, $3.50(number of Italians bought) + $2.70(number of turkeys) = $190

Now we solve using the substitution method:

$x + y = 60$ *so* $x = 60 - y$ *Next we substitute this into the other equation:*

52

$3.50(60 - y) + 2.70(y) = \$190$ *Now we distribute and solve for y:*

$\$210 - 3.50(y) + 2.70(y) = \$190$ $-.80y = -20$ $y = 25$ *turkey sandwiches*

Note: The elimination or graphing techniques to solving systems of equations would have worked here as well.

Alternate Method: Working backwards

Let's say the above problem had given us these five answer choices, just like on an ACT.

a) 20   b) 25   c) 35   d) 40   e) 50

Instead of going through the substitution method, we can work backwards from the answers.

Let's start with answer C (see page 43 to find out why):

If Joe bought 35 turkey sandwiches and paid $2.70 for each one, he spent: $35 \times 2.70 = \$94.50$

But we know Joe bought 60 total sandwiches, so he must have bought 25 Italians too. So he spent $25 \times \$3.50 = \$87.50$ *on those*

In all Joe spent: $\$94.50 + \$87.50 = \$182$ *This is incorrect; we were told he spent $190.*

Now try the same process with the correct answer (25); you will find that Joe spends $190 total.

25) The graph of the equation $y = 2x^2 + 4$ passes through the point (2,3b). What is the value of *b*?

If a graph passes through a point, that point fits back into the equation. To demonstrate:

$y = 2(2^2) + 4$ $y = 12$ *On the graph of this equation, when x = 2, y = 12.*

The graph passes through the point (2,12), so $3b = 12$ *and* **b = 4**

Note: Make sure you understand the concept that a set of points will fit back into its equation. For example: on the line y = 2x+4   (3,10) is a point because 10 = 2(3)+4 ; Another example: on the parabola y = x²+3x+3   (1, 7) is a point because 7 = 1²+3(1)+3

26) At Big State University, all bikes are required to have license plates. The license plates consist of three letters. The same letter cannot be used twice on the same plate. How many different license plates could there possibly be?

On this question we simply multiply the number of letter options for each of the three spots on the plate: *(see page 36 for a short explanation of this question type)*

Number of possible plates: 26 *possible letters* × 25 *possibilities* × 24 *possibilities* = *15,600*

We count down because once a letter is used it cannot be on the plate again and is no longer a possibility. If letters could be reused, the answer would be: $26 \times 26 \times 26 = 17{,}576$.

27) The first three terms of a geometric sequence are 4, 14, and 49. What is the next term?

A geometric sequence is a series of terms that differ by a common multiplier (or *common ratio*). One example would be: 3, 6, 12, 24. This series would have a common multiplier of 2.

To find the common multiplier, we divide two consecutive terms.
$14/4 = 3.5 =$ *the common multiplier*   ($49/14$ *would have worked as well*)

$$49 \times 3.5 = 171.5 \text{ is the next term}$$

28) A circle has a circumference of 55 meters. What is the length, in meters, of a 216° arc on this circle?

There are a few ways to solve this, but the most basic is a ratio:

$$\frac{216° \; arc}{360° \; full \; circle} = \frac{x \; meters \; in \; the \; arc}{55 \; meters \; in \; the \; full \; circle}$$

Cross multiply to get: $216(55) = 360(x)$ $x = \dfrac{11880}{360}$ $x = 33$ *meters*

29) If $\sin\theta = \dfrac{\sqrt{5}}{3}$, and θ is between 90° and 180°, what is $\tan\theta$?

This can be solved two ways. First we will try the graphing method. For this method we make a triangle in the second quadrant and use SOHCAHTOA to solve.

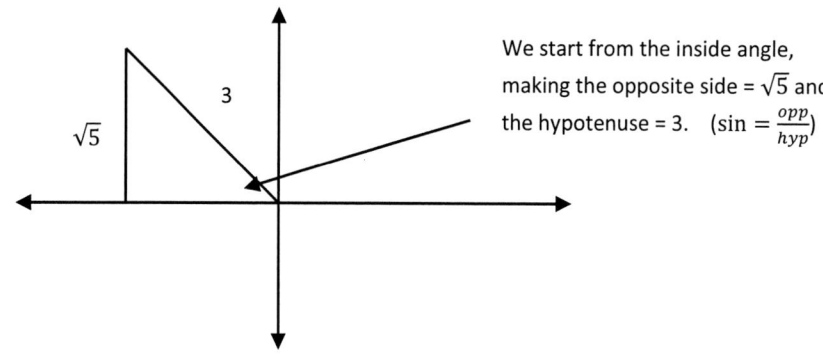

We start from the inside angle, making the opposite side = $\sqrt{5}$ and the hypotenuse = 3. ($\sin = \dfrac{opp}{hyp}$)

We can then fill in the missing side of the triangle using the Pythagorean Theorem:

$$\left(\sqrt{5}\right)^2 + B^2 = 3^2 \qquad 5 + B^2 = 9 \qquad B = 2$$

The diagram now looks like the one below. The 2 is negative because it is going left from the origin (if you use the *all students take calculus* trick you can just determine the sign at the end).

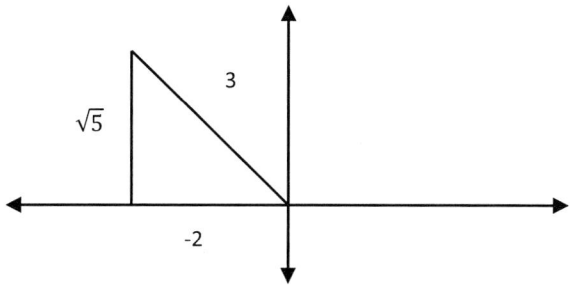

$$\tan\theta = \frac{opp}{adj} \qquad \tan\theta = \frac{\sqrt{5}}{-2}$$

Alternate Method: Use inverses to get the angle on your calculator, and then find tan

$$\sin\theta = \frac{\sqrt{5}}{3} \qquad \theta = \sin^{-1}\frac{\sqrt{5}}{3} \qquad \theta = 48.19 \qquad \tan 48.19 = 1.12$$

1.12 is the same number as $\frac{\sqrt{5}}{2}$. We would have to add the negative sign ourselves based on *all students take calculus*, as the calculator sometimes gives the wrong sign (calculators don't know which quadrant the problem takes place in).

30) If x and y are both > 0, what is $y + \sqrt{\frac{y}{x}}$ equal to?

a) 0 b) $\sqrt{xy}$ c) $\frac{x+y\sqrt{x}}{x^2}$ d) $\frac{y+y\sqrt{x}}{xy}$ e) $\frac{xy+\sqrt{xy}}{x}$

The correct answer is E. Let's see how to do this algebraically.

First, we must know that $\sqrt{\frac{y}{x}} = \frac{\sqrt{y}}{\sqrt{x}}$

Since square roots can cause problems when in the denominator, let's get rid of that right away:

$$\frac{\sqrt{y}}{\sqrt{x}} \times \frac{\sqrt{x}}{\sqrt{x}} = \frac{\sqrt{xy}}{x}$$

The new equation looks like this: $y + \frac{\sqrt{xy}}{x}$

Now we can get a simple common denominator: $\quad y \times \frac{x}{x} = \frac{xy}{x}$

Lastly, we add the fractions to get the answer: $\quad \frac{xy}{x} + \frac{\sqrt{xy}}{x} = \frac{xy+\sqrt{xy}}{x}$

Alternate Method: Dummy numbers

While it is ideal to learn the math behind this problem, we could also solve with 'dummy numbers':

Let's say: $y = 16 \quad x = 4$ *(choose numbers that make the math as simple as possible)*

The equation would be: $y + \sqrt{\frac{y}{x}} = 16 + \sqrt{\frac{16}{4}} = 18$

Now to put the dummies into the answers and see what also equals 18.

a) 0 b) $\sqrt{16(4)} = 8$ c) $\frac{4+16\sqrt{4}}{4^2} = \frac{36}{16}$ d) $\frac{16+16\sqrt{4}}{16(4)} = \frac{48}{64}$ e) $\frac{4(16)+\sqrt{4(16)}}{4} = 18$

Chapter 3 – Reading

Read through this chapter and then take an entire ACT Reading practice test. Use a stopwatch and write down how long it takes you to complete each passage of the test. After doing that, go back through this chapter and use the tips to form a general strategy. If you have never seen an ACT Reading Test, look over a few passages before beginning this chapter.

Format and Basic Strategy

Reading is the third section of the ACT. You are given 35 minutes to read four passages and complete 40 questions (10 per passage) testing your comprehension. The questions are not in any order based on difficulty.

The four passages always come in the following order:

Passage 1 – Prose Fiction: An excerpt from a fictional story

Passage 2 – Social Science: A nonfiction passage based on history or current events

Passage 3 – Humanities: A nonfiction passage usually focusing on the arts (theatre, music, etc.) or an excerpt from a biography

Passage 4 – Natural Science: A nonfiction passage based on science (biology, geology, etc.)

There are two main ACT Reading strategies presented in this book, and both have proved successful for many students. The first strategy is called the 'Reading Method.' This strategy involves carefully reading the passage first, and then completing the questions. The 'Reading Method' is the most popular strategy for the Reading Test. The second strategy is called the 'Look-back Method.' This strategy involves skipping the passage and moving straight to the questions. 'Look-back Method' users simply search through the passage to find each answer; they never actually read the complete text. Both of these methods can work, and the first few sections of this chapter should help you determine your personal approach. **Find what works best for you and get comfortable with it. Everyone has his or her own style for the ACT Reading Test.**

After the strategy sections are separate sections of tips and tricks for those using the Reading Method and those using the Look-Back Method. The two methods require slightly different skills, so each method has its own set of tips. You will find more information about the two methods over the first eight pages of this chapter.

The Foolproof way to Improve your Reading Score

Before getting into the strategies and tips for the ACT Reading Test, I'd like to give one of the most obvious and effective ways to improve your score. It is, simply, to read more. Read the newspaper, a magazine (one with actual articles), or any book. Even spending just 10 minutes a day reading can greatly improve your score, as well as get you prepared for college.

If you do not improve your general reading comprehension, you will find it difficult to make large improvements on this test. While practice tests are great, it takes an overall commitment to being a stronger reader to succeed on the ACT Reading Test.

Most of this book focuses solely on ways to improve your ACT score, but being a good reader is far more important than just achieving a high test score. In any college class or future career, you will be expected to read things and truly understand what the author is trying to say. If you struggle with this, the only way to improve is through practice. So, grab a newspaper or magazine and read one or two serious articles each day. Pick out an interesting book from the library and try to read it over the next month. Look up words you don't know (Bonus: having a good vocabulary makes you sound smart!). Take your time and make sure you really understand what the text is saying. It will pay off throughout your future and, in the meantime, it will help your ACT score too.

Note: Students who read outside of school also see improvements in their ACT English Test scores.

Check out page 77 for a bonus section on improving reading comprehension skills.

To Read or Not to Read

The ACT Reading Test can be approached in many different ways. As mentioned in the introduction, there is not one strategy that is best for everybody. You must find a style that works for you. The most important strategic aspect to determine is whether you will read the passage prior to doing the questions (the 'Reading Method'), or if you will skip straight to the questions and rely on looking back in the text to find answers (the 'Look-Back Method'). Later I will discuss some ways you can mix reading and not reading, but usually students pick one way or the other.

If you can pull it off, the best technique is to read the passage carefully and then move on to the questions (the 'Reading Method'). Reading is the only way you can consistently score higher than 28 on this section. When you truly understand the passage, the questions cannot fool you all that much. However, many students (at least 50%) have some problems with reading first. The most common complaints are that the passage is too boring to follow, the passage is too hard to understand, and the passage takes too long to read. These are valid concerns, but sometimes they can be overcome. It is not easy, though, and improving general reading skills takes time. Let's address the three common concerns one by one.

The passage is too boring – Yes, ACT passages are not usually very exciting. Throughout your life, though, you will be forced to read things that are not all that interesting. Get used to it! Get focused and make an effort to get your mind centered on the text. You cannot treat these readings like they are a chore – a relaxed, upbeat attitude is important.

For example, say a reading passage is about the French Monarch Louis XIV. Even if you have zero interest in the subject, you must stay interested and positive in order to understand and remember the text. After reading the first paragraph, don't think "ughh, I hate history." Then your mind is bound to wander, and chances are that you will comprehend very little. A more effective attitude would be "alright, this old guy did some crazy things; let's see what this is all about." That positive, relaxed attitude will help you immensely as you read through the text. Yes, you may be lying to yourself (maybe you really do hate history), but it only takes three to five minutes to get through a passage. **If you can stay interested for just a few minutes, your comprehension will improve greatly.**

Note: Practice pays off. Pick out one boring-looking newspaper article a day and read it for comprehension. You will notice improvement in your reading skills in just a week or two.

The passage is too hard to understand – This is the most common and valid reason why students choose not to read the passage prior to doing the questions. These passages are not written for kids; they are taken from newspapers, serious magazines, scholarly journals, and various types of fictional and nonfictional books. That said, if you are taking the ACT, you are no longer a kid, and you will only see more articles like these as you progress to college. As I mentioned earlier, the key to improving your skills is practice. If you commit to developing your reading skills and vocabulary, you will eventually have no problem understanding these passages. Work at it a little each day and you will see gradual improvement. Even if you choose to skip the reading and go straight to the questions (the 'Look-Back Method'), being a strong reader helps greatly when you are looking for answers in the text.

It takes too long to read it – The ACT Reading Test is a race to the finish – at least 80% of students have some issue with time. However, the issue is never solely the time it takes to read the passage. The issue is the combination of reading time and comprehension.

You get an average of 8 minutes and 45 seconds to complete each passage. A typical reader might finish the text in about 3 minutes and 45 seconds, giving her 5 minutes to complete the questions. However, say you are not the quickest reader, and you take 4 minutes and 45 seconds to read, giving you 4 minutes to complete the questions. This is not necessarily a problem. If you truly understand the passage and remember important facts, you will have no issues finishing the questions on time. Now let's say you speed through the text in 2 minutes, but you remember nothing and did not even pinpoint the main idea of the passage. Those 2 minutes would be a complete waste of time. Reading time is all relative to how much of the text you understand. You must find the balance between speed and comprehension.

Therefore, you may want to find ways to improve your reading speed without sacrificing comprehension. Again, the best way is to simply practice reading regularly. If you challenge yourself to read every day, you will get faster.

Here are a few other ways to improve your reading speed: (use with caution! make sure you've mastered a technique before using it on the ACT)

- Try not to mouth the words to yourself as you read (keep your lips shut).
- Avoid saying the unimportant words to yourself in your head (this takes a lot of practice!). Train yourself to pay more attention to meaningful words.
- Try to focus most on the middle words – limit eye movement by letting your peripheral vision pick up the words on the right and left edges
- As you read, follow the text with your pencil – keep pressing yourself to move faster while still understanding the text

These are only basic techniques, but more advanced information on speed reading can easily be found online (some YouTube videos on the subject are quite good). Just don't overdo it; too much speed reading can backfire. **Understanding the text is much more important than reading it quickly.**

So... To Read or not to Read?

Every student should aim to become a strong enough reader to be able to read these passages, understand them, and then do the questions. However, becoming that strong of a reader can be difficult and time consuming. In the meantime, some students will perform best by skipping straight to the questions and searching back into the text to find each answer. While I encourage the Reading Method, the Look-Back Method can work well. Some Look-Back Method students consistently score in the mid to high 20s, and scores of 30+ are not completely out of the question.

So which way works best for you? To determine the answer, first read through the rest of this chapter. The next section gets deeper into strategy, which should help you shape your personal approach to the ACT Reading Test. After that there are separate sections of tips and tricks for those who use the Reading Method and for those who use the Look-Back Method. Try checking out both, especially if you are still unsure which method you will use. Finally, when you finish with the Reading section of this book, grab a couple of practice tests and try both methods. You will quickly find which style is more comfortable and effective for you.

Bonus Strategy – Combining the Reading Method and Look-Back Method

A small percentage of students perform best when they use the Reading Method on some passages, and the Look-Back Method on others. Again, read through this section and take practice tests to determine your own technique. The following are some of the ways students combine these methods.

- A common combination of the methods is to use the Reading Method for the *Prose Fiction* passage (passage 1), and the Look-Back Method for the other three passages. The Look-Back Method can sometimes be problematic in *Prose Fiction*, as you find yourself looking back to the middle of a story and having no idea what has happened, who the characters are, etc. Students using this strategy will sometimes save the *Prose Fiction* passage for last so they know exactly how much time is remaining. Check out the upcoming *General Tips, Tricks, and Strategies* section for more on saving passages for last and effective time management.

- Another combination similar to the first is to use the Reading Method for *Prose Fiction* and *Humanities* (passages 1 and 3), and the Look-Back Method for *Social Science* and *Natural Science* (passages 2 and 4). *Humanities* usually is not as full of complicated facts as the Science passages are, and sometimes it is an easy-reading story (similar to *Prose Fiction*). Usually students who choose this method are decent readers, but are not scientific minded and have trouble comprehending all the facts in the Science passages.

- The final and most common combination is to use the Reading Method on each of the first three passages, and then use the Look-Back Method on the fourth (*Natural Science*). Most often this is used simply because the student is running out of time! The *Natural Science* passage is full of scientific facts, and you can usually look up a few answers even with limited time remaining. If you find yourself low on time, it may be best to use the Look-Back Method on passage 4. More on this strategy appears on page 65.

These are the most common techniques, but you can use any combination of strategies that works well for you on practice tests. As mentioned in the introduction, everyone has to find his or her own style for the ACT Reading Test. But beware; **most students find that a nice, simple strategy works better than switching things up too much.**

Note: Even if you choose to use the Look-Back Method at first, do not completely give up on the Reading Method. With practice you can develop your reading skills.

Reading – General Tips, Tricks, and Strategies

As the last section indicated, the number one decision to be made is whether to use the 'Reading Method' or the 'Look-Back Method.' Whichever you choose, you may want to incorporate these additional strategies into your approach to the Reading Test.

1. ***Save the Worst for Last***

    It is always beneficial to do the passage that is hardest for you last. In this case, if you run out of time, you will have already completed your better passages. The two passages that give students the most problems are *Prose Fiction* and *Natural Science*. The other passages <u>usually</u> are a bit easier than these two. Take practice tests to determine which passage tends to be the hardest for you.

    Many students find *Natural Science* the most difficult because it usually contains the toughest vocabulary and most confusing language. *Natural Science* already is the last passage, so you do not need to change the order if it is the most difficult for you.

    Prose Fiction is different than the other passages in that you work with a story instead of nonfictional information. If you find interpreting the story to be more difficult or time consuming than the other passages, then do *Prose Fiction* last. If you choose to do *Prose Fiction* last, you will start with passage 2 (*Social Science*) and then come back to passage 1 after you have finished all the others.

    Note: Every ACT Reading Test is different. Don't rush to immediately pick your "worst" passage, as you may have just hit one particularly difficult version. Over time, figure out which passage type generally gives you the most trouble, and save that one for last.

2. ***Taking it Straight***

    If you have absolutely no issues completing the Reading Test in the given 35 minutes, you do not need to 'Save the Worst for Last.' Simply take the test in its given order. This gives you an average of 8 minutes and 45 seconds to complete each passage – not an easy task, but it certainly can be done. Keep in mind that you only need to <u>average</u> 8 minutes and 45 seconds. Sometimes one passage takes 10 minutes to complete, while an easier one takes 7 minutes. As long as you have tried practice tests and proven that you can finish on time, don't worry if you take an extra minute on the occasional passage.

3. ***The 10 10 10 5 and Related Strategies***

    This is a great strategy for people who struggle to complete the Reading Test on time. First, use the tips above to determine which passage you will do last. Next, determine how long it takes you to complete a passage (grab a stopwatch and write down your times on a few practice passages). You want to complete the passages comfortably, but don't act like you have unlimited time. Even if you struggle with time, a solid, attainable goal is ten minutes per passage.

Now '10 10 10 5' is pretty self-explanatory. Spend roughly ten minutes on each of your stronger passages, then five on your weakest. You don't need to watch the clock on every passage, but try to get comfortable finishing in the nine to eleven minute range. Even if you take eleven minutes on each of your first three passages, you still have two minutes to make guesses on the final passage. Don't worry if you completely bomb one passage as long as you worked hard on the other three. **You can get 10 questions wrong and still finish with a 25 – 28 in Reading.** Strategies like this one show the importance of completing a couple of practice Reading Tests. You want to have a plan before you take the official ACT.

But how do you approach the final passage when you only have two to six minutes to complete it? The next strategy gives two options that will allow you to get some correct answers even with very limited time.

4. *Running Out of Time Strategy*

Whether you have used a strategy like '10 10 10 5' or attempted to take the test in a standard fashion, you may find yourself running low on time as you near the end of the test. Time management is an issue for most students, and it can be a difficult problem to overcome. If you find yourself having serious problems with time, you can improve with practice and by using other methods described throughout this chapter. Also, always remember that doing three passages well and guessing on the fourth can still result in a solid score.

If you are running behind, stay relaxed, finish as much as you can, and guess on any remaining questions. If you hurry to get everything done too quickly you will end up with a lot of wrong answers. The following are techniques for when you are running out of time, divided into advice for those who use the Look-back Method and those who use the Reading Method.

Look-Back Method – When time gets short, the most important thing is to stay calm and keep on task. You should not change your basic strategy – keep the same style and follow the tips presented on pages 78 to 83. The only difference is that now you should be a bit pickier about which questions to complete. If a question seems difficult or time-consuming, just take a guess and move on. Maximize your score by completing as many easy questions as possible. *Tip 2 on page 78 goes deeper into question choice.*

Reading Method – If time is running low for the final passage, you have two options.

    a. *The Read and Go*

        Depending on the amount of time you have remaining, either skim or read the passage. Then get down to business on the questions. Do them quickly with a minimal amount of looking back into the text. Don't waste time on difficult or time-consuming questions. The goal is to get as many right answers as possible, but you probably don't have time to get every single one correct. This strategy works best for skilled readers who can get a solid understanding of the passage in one read. If you choose this option, *Tip 3*, 'Stick to the Main Idea,' will be essential to completing the questions accurately in limited time (see page 68).

    b. *Become a 'Look-Backer'*

        This is generally the better option, especially if you have less than five or six minutes left. When time is running low, the Look-Back Method can help you snag a few valuable points in the last moments. Learning the basics of the Look-Back Method is easy – check out the tips on pages 78 to 83. If you do plan on using this strategy, set a time as to when you will read, and when you will switch to Look-Back. For example, if you have less than six minutes remaining for the final passage you will use Look-Back; if you have more time than that you will read. Having a set time keeps you prepared and relaxed.

Note: Keep in mind that the Look-Back Method tends to work better on the Natural Science passage than on any of the other three. The Natural Science passage usually has fewer 'big picture questions' than the other three passages. Many Natural Science questions can be completed without knowledge of the passage's overall themes and main ideas.

The Reading Method –Tips, Tricks, and Strategies

READING TIPS – These tips will help with your initial read through the passage.

1. ***Make the First Read Count***

    If you are taking the time to read the entire passage, it is important that you get good information out of your efforts. Here are a few tips to make sure your first read through is productive:

    - *Find your Pace*

    The Reading Test is a race against the clock, but that doesn't mean you have to read the passage at 100 miles per hour. Many students try to read so quickly that they really do not understand the text. **If you do not understand the passage, then you are wasting your time**. Of course, you cannot go too slowly, but don't worry if it takes a little extra reading time to truly comprehend the passage. Taking an extra 30 seconds on your first read can save time in the long run. You will easily make that time up when you cruise through the questions with your solid knowledge of the text. Usually it is time spent searching back into the text for answers that makes you fall behind pace, not time spent reading the passage.

    - *Get Interested in the Passage*

    Think about reading your favorite magazine. If you are a sports fan, you read a *Sports Illustrated* article and remember every statistic. If you like music, you can remember every story in the latest *Rolling Stone*. Now think about reading a boring newspaper article. If you are not interested in politics, you read about the presidential race and do not remember one thing from the article. The point is that we remember things we read if we have interest in the subject.

    ACT Reading passages are probably more similar to a boring newspaper article than your favorite magazine. They are short passages, though, and if you can trick yourself into being interested for just a few minutes, you will remember much more of the content. So, start reading with a good attitude. Try pretending the passage is a chapter in the best book you have ever read. Perhaps think to yourself "Wow! I want to learn more about this" after reading the first paragraph. **Do whatever it takes to stay interested and focused** – it will pay off when you get to the questions.

- *Pretend you are giving a speech*

99% of students say the words in their head as they read ACT Reading passages. And due to the pressure of the test, most students say these words to themselves like a robot! They say everything in the same monotone voice (in their head) and do not stress important information or pause at key spots. This does not help comprehension at all. As you say the words to yourself, pretend you are giving a speech. Change your tone when an exclamation is made. Pause when the author uses a dash to stress key information. If you read the text like you are giving a speech – and not like you are a robot – your comprehension will improve greatly.

Note: Try this tip on a couple of practice passages before using it on the official ACT Test. It is a simple technique, but it still takes a little bit of practice.

- *Slow Down or Read Back when Necessary*

Even when trying to stay interested, your mind is bound to wander every once in a while. **If your thoughts drift off or your mind goes blank (you stop thinking about the material), do not continue reading. Stop for a second and get refocused on the passage.** You may even want to skim back a few sentences to pick up anything you missed while your thoughts were elsewhere. It is important to stay on track while reading these passages. If you don't pay attention for just one paragraph, you may find yourself completely lost.

Additionally, sometimes students start to lose track of the passage because a couple of sentences are confusing. Again, stop and skim back when this happens. Try to understand what the sentences are saying with context clues (what the other sentences in that paragraph say). You do not need to understand every little detail in a passage, but if you lose sight of the big picture, you will be in trouble when you reach the questions. Taking extra time to read and reread will pay off if it helps you understand the passage.

2. ***The Goals of the First Read***

As the last tip indicated, **the primary goal of the first read is to truly understand the big picture of the passage.** While picking up on details is great, it is most important to gain a grasp of the main ideas presented in the text. **The next most important thing to understand is the tone of the author.** The tone is how the author feels about the subject and the basic way he or she goes about explaining it. The tone goes hand-in-hand with the main ideas; if you really understand the passage, you will be able to connect the main ideas to the author's tone. **Finally, you want to form an idea of the progression of the essay**, so when you go back to look for an answer, you know where to look. I'll explain each of these goals in detail in the next few tips.

3. *Stick to the Main Idea*

Finding the main idea of each passage will give a major clue to answering roughly half of the Reading Test questions. Usually three to six questions per passage directly relate to the passage's main point(s). This is not to say that ACT asks "What is the main idea of the passage?" twenty times per test, but **even questions about small details often relate to the big picture of the passage**.

For example, a recent ACT Test contained a passage about a woman returning to the town she grew up in. When she returns, she is disappointed to find that the old farm village has become much more modern. The following question is based on that passage.

According to the narrator, which store has come most recently to her hometown?

A. The Corner Bookstore
B. Old Bill's Grocery
C. The Computer Warehouse
D. The Fishing Shop

Even without evidence from a passage, I am sure that C is the correct answer. As I mentioned, the theme of the passage is that the woman is upset about her old farm town being modernized. It is very logical that "The Computer Warehouse" would be one of the new, modern additions to the town. Choices A, B, and D all sound like stores that would fit in an old farm village; these stores have probably been around for a while.

Many students are tempted to search back into the passage to find the answer on a question like the one above, but that would be a waste of time. When only one answer fits the main idea of the passage, you do not need to prove it in the text. My general rule is as follows: **if you are at least 75% sure an answer is correct, just go with it**. You simply do not have the time to prove every answer in the text. Of course, the 75% number can be adjusted slightly based on your time management skills and target score.

Note: As an exercise, read a practice passage and write down its main idea or argument in a maximum of two sentences. Now try doing the questions with your sentence(s) in front of you. Try this again on a few more passages. Eventually you will not need the sentences; focusing on the main idea will become automatic.

Note: If you are having trouble pinpointing the main idea, look to the first and last paragraphs of the essay. The writer often establishes the main idea early in the passage and revisits it in the conclusion.

4. ***Stick to the Main Idea Part 2 – Within the Passage***

Sometimes the Reading Test contains questions about one specific paragraph or a secondary theme to the passage. Take the same focus on the main idea; just apply it on a smaller scale.

For example, say a passage focuses on the debate between more taxation for better schools and roads, or less taxation so Americans can save money. Here is a short paragraph taken from the passage followed by a question that relates to it:

Some economists argue that income taxes are unfair to those who do not have children in public schools or regularly use the highway system. Bill Evans, a professor at Big State University says, "Advanced toll systems have created a way to shift burdens to those who utilize the asset in question, which should be the goal of most forms of taxation."….

Based on his quote, Bill Evans most likely would support:

A. Higher tax rates for people with children in public schools.
B. One tax rate for all people.
C. Tax breaks for large families.
D. An increase in the overall tax rate.

The correct answer is A. Bill Evans' quote is tough to understand, but we really do not need it at all. The first sentence of the paragraph says that we are hearing from people who think income taxes are unfair to a certain set of people. This is the main idea of the paragraph, and choice A fits right in with this theme. Just as in the previous tip, you want to keep in mind the bigger picture as you answer the question. As I will explain further in *Tip 8*, don't limit yourself just to Bill Evans' quote (even though that is what the question mentions) – read around it to obtain a better understanding of the big picture.

Note: As an exercise, read through a practice passage one paragraph at a time. After reading each paragraph, jot down its main idea without looking back at the text. If you can pull some solid information from every paragraph, you will be in great shape when you get to the questions. This is also an effective way to improve general reading skills.

5. *Tone Tells*

Tone refers to both the author's attitude about the subject and his style of writing about it. If your reading skills are very good, you will notice tone without even thinking about it; if you need some work on reading, concentrating just a little bit on tone will improve your overall comprehension.

Here are just a few examples of tone you will see in ACT Reading passages:

- A scientific approach to explaining the subject of the passage
- A symbolic, artsy approach to explaining the passage
- Admiration for the people involved in the passage
- Anger over an issue

Just as with main ideas, you may find a couple of different tones within a single passage. For example, say a few paragraphs of an essay focus on pollution in our seas (author takes an angry tone), and another paragraph focuses on new technologies to clean water (author takes a cautiously hopeful tone). While recognizing tone will help you most with overall comprehension, it also can be directly applied to some ACT Reading questions. Often tone helps you eliminate wrong answers, and sometimes it confirms a correct answer.

On a recent ACT, an author spoke about different systems of classifying animals and other objects. He had an excited tone; he found these classifications to be helpful in organizing things. The following question is based on that passage.

A house painter typically divides the jobs he receives into two categories, "simple jobs" and "complex jobs," based on his first look over of the home. Based on this passage, how would the author portray this classification technique?

A. Objective and able to be redone by coworkers
B. Unimportant and not helpful to the painter
C. Unofficial and not scientific enough
D. Useful and significant to the painter

The correct answer is D. Based purely off the question, answers B, C, and D could be considered true; however, we have to take the author's tone into account. As I mentioned, he is excited about classification systems. His tone suggests that he would see some value in the painter using this simple system to organize his jobs.

Note (Important!): When analyzing answer choices, think to yourself, "Does this sound like something the author would say?" If it does not, it probably is a wrong answer.

6. *Know Your Characters / Subjects*

Just as we keep in mind the author's feelings and ideas, we also want to concentrate on the personalities of the characters / subjects of the passage. Let's look at how this tip applies to each passage:

Prose Fiction – Because this passage is a story (or a small part of a story), knowing the characters is especially important. If you truly know who everybody is, their basic personalities, and the major facts about them, you will be in great shape to answer the *Prose Fiction* questions. Pay extra attention when a character is described. Don't hesitate to slow down and/or look back in the text if you lose track of who is who in a passage.

For example, a recent *Prose Fiction* passage gave the story of a young man's life. The man in the passage, Tim, is a shy, gentle, modest man. In the passage he meets a quiet, humble young woman named Jane. They both are in the same poetry writing class. The following question is based on that passage.

In the passage, the notion that Jane's poetry is straightforward, yet beautiful is best described as the idea of:

A. Tim that he mentions to Jane to excite her
B. Tim that he thinks about after hearing her work
C. Jane that she announces to the rest of the class
D. Jane that she argues with the teacher about

The correct answer is B. Answers A, C, and D do not fit with the personalities of the characters. Tim is shy and gentle, and it's unlikely he would be using pick up lines on Jane! Jane is quiet and humble, not the type of person who brags about her work or gets in arguments with teachers. The only answer that agrees with the characters' personalities is that Tim quietly formed the idea after hearing her poetry.

Note: In this example, I directly told you about each character. In a passage you will have to figure out the character traits from descriptions, actions, thoughts, and dialogue. As you practice Fiction passages, make a point to look for these things and underline them. This will get you in the habit of paying special attention to the characters.

Note: Not everyone is a major character. If someone seems like a minor player in the passage, it may not be worth concentrating on him or her.

Social Science – The *Social Science* passage generally focuses on a person, event, or social issue. If it focuses mainly on one person, it is essential to recognize who the person is and what the person stands for. Even if you know the facts, your understanding is incomplete if you do not get an idea of the subject's personality. If there are a few people mentioned, just try to keep track of who is who and find each person's basic beliefs. Again, do not overdo it with minor characters. If people seem unimportant to the passage, don't waste too much time on them.

Humanities – *Humanities* sometimes reads like a story, and sometimes is more similar to a *Social Science* passage. Either way, the goal is to be able to describe every important character / subject when you finish the passage.

Natural Science – The *Natural Science* passage usually does not have many important people involved. It is more likely to talk about plants, animals, or something else out of a science book. However, you often hear opinions from a few different scientists in the passage. If you can pick up the basic ideas of each scientist as you read, that is ideal. If you have trouble keeping all these people straight, consider underlining their names as you initially read the passage (you can also underline their basic arguments if time permits). In that case, when you look back to the text while answering a question, you will be able to find people and their ideas quickly.

Note: As I mentioned before, everyone has his or her own style for the Reading Test. Practice all of these techniques and find which ones help you the most.

QUESTION TIPS – *After you have finished reading, use these tips to help you accurately complete the questions.*

7. ***If it Sounds "A Little Wrong," it Probably is Wrong***

    ACT tries to trick you by giving answer choices that are partly correct, but also contain a few words that just do not fit. These choices are tempting because they do have some truth to them. But be careful! If even a small part of an answer is wrong, the whole answer is wrong. Here is an excerpt from a passage and an example:

    > Kyle saw Jim McCafrey, the carefree music shop owner, as an idol and mentor. Despite the fact that they had not talked in many years, Kyle was more excited and anxious to see Jim than any of his old friends. When Kyle was a teenager, McCafrey first showed him how to play the piano, instilling in him a deep appreciation for all types of music. Twenty years later Kyle was considered one of the greatest rock and roll pianists in the country. Kyle began to feel his nerves as he stepped into the music shop.

Which of the following most accurately describes the upcoming meeting between Kyle and Jim McCafrey?

A. Kyle is nervous about seeing Jim McCafrey because he is unsure if he can live up to Jim's expectations.
B. Despite being nervous about an upcoming concert, Kyle is excited to see his old mentor Jim McCafrey.
C. Despite being a famous pianist, Kyle is overcome with emotion when it comes to meeting Jim McCafrey several years after their last contact.
D. Kyle is worried that Jim McCafrey might be upset because Kyle has not contacted him since becoming a famous musician.

The correct answer is C. All the other options contain some truth, but also contain a few words that are clearly wrong. Choice A says Kyle is unsure if he can live up to Jim's expectations. This is incorrect because Kyle is a very well-regarded pianist and Jim is characterized as a carefree person. Choice B says Kyle is nervous about an upcoming concert, which is not found anywhere in the text. Choice D is wrong because nothing suggests that McCafrey is upset at Kyle. Choice C is the only 100% correct answer.

Note: Use this tip to eliminate choices quickly and improve your time. Of course, you need to be careful: you don't want to eliminate every single answer choice! Just watch out for words that are clearly incorrect and avoid settling on partly right answers.

*Note: **Often answer choices can be eliminated just because they do not match up with the author's tone in the essay** (remember Tip 5).*

8. *Don't Only Read the Lines They Mention*

Usually about two to five questions per passage mention some line numbers. For example, the question would say "From the quote in lines 40-44..." or "The term in line 18 refers to..." While it is fastest to choose an answer without referring back to the text, you will usually need to look back on this question type. Actually, these questions are not too time-consuming to look up in the text, as the question tells you right where to look!

The key on these 'line number questions' is a simple technique: don't focus only on the line(s) mentioned in the question. Read around the mentioned lines and get some context for the part of the passage the question is asking about (that is, figure out what the other sentences nearby are saying). A little extra reading on these questions will aid your performance immensely. The next tip elaborates on this further.

9. ***Looking for Answers in the Text***

Ideally, you will know the answers to the questions based on your careful read of the passage, knowledge of tone and main idea, and familiarity with subjects/characters. But, of course, you will run into some questions that ask about something you did not pick up on during the first read. On these questions you have to search back into the text. When searching back, the key is to be fast and accurate. Let's look at how to accomplish each of these goals.

Finding Answers Fast

If you spent 3 minutes and 45 seconds reading the text, you have an average of 30 seconds to answer each question in order to stay on pace. Now remember, some questions take longer than others, and some passages take longer than others, so don't obsess over the 30 seconds. Nonetheless, you do have to be quick on the ACT Reading Test.

One thing that slows people down is spending a lot of time searching through the text to find answers to questions. Here are some methods to speed up your search:

a. **Helpers for your Search**

When searching for answers, you want to look for words and punctuation that will catch your eye quickly. Some things are particularly easy to spot: capitalized proper nouns, unusual words, very long words, quotation marks, numbers, and dates.

If possible, tailor your searches to looking for easily noticed words. For example, if a question asks about stadiums in Norway, you would search for the word *Norway* (capitalized proper noun), not the word *stadium*. Or if the answer choices are all dates (1942, August 30, etc.) from the text, look for these before you look for anything in the question. Finding the dates will be faster than skimming for a few words from the question.

b. **Remember the Progression**

After reading the passage, you should have some idea of the progression of ideas. The following is an example of a typical essay's progression.

1st paragraph – Introduction – Is football surpassing baseball as "America's game"?

2nd and 3rd paragraph – Facts about football's rising popularity

4th and 5th – Experts who believe football has surpassed baseball

6th and 7th – Facts saying baseball is still our favorite sport

8th – Expert opinion saying baseball is still on top

9th – Conclusion – It depends how you look at it

Let's say a question read "How much higher are television ratings for football games than for baseball games?" You would start looking for the answer somewhere around the 2nd paragraph. If a question asked about baseball great Yogi Berra's opinion, you would probably look at the 8th paragraph. ACT passages are skillfully written and every one of them will be well organized. When going back to find an answer, try to remember the progression and use it to speed up your search.

c. **The Mighty First Paragraph**

More answers come from the first paragraph than any other, particularly in the *Science* passages (passages 2 and 4). If a question asks about general, preliminary information, the answer is probably found in or near the first paragraph.

For example, say we have a passage about the migration of a breed of birds. A question about any of these facts would most likely be answered near the beginning of the essay:

- Where the birds originate from and where they go
- The amount of time the journey takes
- The birds' size, species, and physical characteristics

d. **Check the Choices and Eliminate** *(optional)*

Even if you are sure you need to look back to the text to answer a question, consider checking out the answer choices prior to looking back. You may be able to eliminate some choices right away, as usually one or two will not make sense given the main ideas and tone of the essay. Once you have eliminated a choice or two, keep the remaining choices in mind as you go back to the text. If you know your options you can quickly confirm which one is correct.

e. **Don't Search at All! (The 75% Rule)**

Resist the urge to look up every single answer. If you are at least 75% confident in an answer choice, just go with it. You can always circle the question and come back later if you have extra time. This tip is especially important on questions that will take a long time to find in the text. If you find yourself clueless as to where an answer would be found, it may be smart to just go with the answer that fits with the main ideas and tone of the essay.

Once the Answer is Within Sight

When searching back for an answer, it is important to find the necessary text quickly. It is even more important to accurately interpret the text and choose the correct answer. Often students find the part of the passage they are searching for, find text nearby that resembles an answer choice, and then choose that answer without thinking. If you have done this, the ACT pulled one of its favorite tricks on you. The ACT often gives answer choices that look correct at first glance, but can be proved wrong with just a few seconds of reading. The lesson: **When you find the part of the passage you need to answer a question – stop, read, and think. You are 70% of the way to the right answer; don't rush it now! The goal is not to just find words. The goal is to understand them.** So take your time and do what is necessary to understand the text. You will often need to read extra information to get some context. Taking just a few extra seconds can be the difference between a right and wrong answer. Here is an example to illustrate this tip. Try this one working backwards; start with the question, and then look back to the text to find the answer.

Mathew Brady's photography stands as the preeminent work documenting the American Civil War. While his work garnered some popularity many years later, the public had little interest in his images when they were first released. The grim realities of his photos did not resonate with people who were understandably weary after four years of intense and deadly war. After investing his entire fortune in the noble pursuit of documenting the war, Brady was devastated.

Based on the passage, how did people react to Mathew Brady's photography just after the Civil War?

A. The work gained popularity, and then people lost interest
B. People were tired of war, and thus did not care for the photography
C. The photos were popular, but some people found the work too grim
D. The photos were too expensive, so people did not like them

The correct answer is B. Answers A, C, and D do match up to certain sections of the text, but they simply do not answer the question correctly. Slowly reread the second and third sentences of the paragraph if you answered incorrectly. Look up any words you do not know – this level of vocabulary is standard on ACT passages. Once you truly understand sentences two and three, you see that choice B is the only correct option.

Note: For more help on looking up answers in the text, check out the tips for the Look-Back Method on pages 78 – 83.

Bonus Power Page: Improving Reading Comprehension Skills

In the end, the failsafe way to improve your ACT Reading score is by developing strong reading comprehension skills. If you understand the passage's big picture and remember key facts, the questions really cannot fool you. Here are a few techniques to become a better reader: *Practice these techniques by applying them on any book, magazine, newspaper, etc.*

Visualization: This doesn't mean closing your eyes and looking out into space for ten seconds. But taking a moment to get a quick mental picture helps immensely. The passage becomes more 'real' and events begin to fit together.

Note: Feel like this requires too much imagination? Some of the best mental pictures are adaptations of things you've seen in movies, pictures, or real life.

Make personal connections: When you read something with a connection to your life, take note of it. This will make facts more memorable and improve your focus. For example, music is commonly a theme in ACT Reading passages. Everyone, from a marching band member to a casual hip-hop fan, can make a personal connection to music. Particularly, a recent ACT Reading passage focused on a man's love of opera music. While you may not listen to opera, you can still identify with the strong feelings the character showed towards music and how it played a major role in his life. Those identifications will lead to better comprehension.

Make connections within the passage: *Important!* As mentioned before, grasping the 'big picture' of the passage is essential. One key way to do this is by making connections within the passage. The ACT Reading Test contains well-written, coherent passages. Don't treat them like a bunch of unrelated paragraphs. For example, say one paragraph explains how organic apples are difficult to grow due to pests. Then the next paragraph talks about the high cost of organic apples. A good reader would tie these things together and make a simple connection: 'organic apples are probably expensive because they are difficult to grow.' It sounds obvious, but if you don't consciously take a mental note while reading, it can slip right past you. This leads to the next technique…

Keep your mind alert and THINK about what you are reading: Take a second to summarize the information when it's getting overwhelming. Think 'WHY is this happening?' Obviously you don't want to drift too far from the text, but a little thought about the passage will help it all make sense.

Make predictions: The simple action of predicting what the author will say next demonstrates a level of focus that leads to strong comprehension. Whether your prediction is right or wrong isn't important.

Have fun: Be easily impressed! For example, a recent ACT passage focused on the building of the Erie Canal (a waterway in New York), and the subject could be interpreted two ways: as a boring river built in the 1800s, or as an amazing accomplishment that made New York City the economic capital of the USA. Guess which outlook would lead to better comprehension...

The Look-Back Method – Tips, Tricks, and Strategies

Many students find their best option is to skip reading the passages, and instead jump straight into the questions. This method tends to help with time management and, when done well, can still lead to scores in the mid to high 20s. While this option seems simple (read the question, find the answer), there are several strategies to help your accuracy.

1. *Decide if you Want to Read Anything*

    Most students who choose the 'Look-Back Method' simply go straight to the questions without spending any time reading the passage. A smaller percentage prefer to read the first paragraph of the essay (and sometimes the last paragraph too) to get some background information. Others like to read the first sentences of each paragraph to get an idea of the progression of the essay, and then move on to the questions. All these tactics can work, as long as you get something productive out of your reading time. Practice and see what works for you.

    Most Look-Back Method students find that no reading at all is most effective for them. While reading first paragraphs and/or sentences can help sometimes, usually these tactics end up being time wasters. Furthermore, I do not recommend the strategy of skimming the entire passage and then going on to the questions. This almost always ends up being a waste of time, as students usually get very little legitimate information from skimming.

2. *Choose Question Order Wisely – Don't Start with Number One!*

    When using the Look-Back Method, do not answer the questions in their given order. Answer questions that relate to small, easy to look-up details first. After completing these, you will know a bit about the passage, and will be ready to complete questions about the overall themes of the essay (the 'big picture questions'). Here are a few guidelines about which questions to attack first:

    - First go to 'line-number questions.' Line-number questions actually mention certain line numbers from the passage. They will say something like "Based on the quote in lines 36 – 39..." or "The word in line 45..." There are about two to five of these per passage, and they usually are based on just a small area of the text. You do not need an understanding of the entire passage to complete these questions, so they are an ideal place to begin. Additionally, sometimes questions ask about entire paragraphs (they may say something like, "Based on the second paragraph..."). It is OK to do these in the beginning as well. Reading entire paragraphs will improve your overall understanding of the passage, which will be important as you progress to more general questions.

- Next, look for short questions and/or short answer choices. Typically, shorter questions and answers are focused on facts from the essay and require less interpretation. Since you may still be shaky on the main themes and ideas of the essay, it is better to simply find facts first. Also, look for questions that say the words "According to the passage." These tend to be based off facts found in the passage as well.

- Now you should have only a few questions remaining. At this point you can't get too particular – just pick a question and go with it. Hopefully, after completing the fact-based questions, you have read enough that you have some understanding of the big picture of the essay. Now the more general questions will not be as difficult.

Note: Clearly mark your answers in your test booklet so you know which questions you have done and which you still have to complete. Be careful with your answer sheet too!

Note: Check out pages 147 – 152 to see examples of changing the question order. (You will need to download ACT Form 64E from ACTPowerPrep.com as well)

3. ***Looking for Answers in the Text***

Note: Some of this information is reprinted from the Reading Method tips on pages 74 – 76. It is worth rereading, though, as looking up answers is what the Look-Back Method is all about.

To successfully complete questions with the Look-Back Method, you must be able to find the necessary text, interpret it, and determine an accurate answer. The following tips focus on those three tasks. Read this section carefully; these techniques are the backbone of the Look-Back Method.

Finding the Necessary Information

If you spent no time reading, you have an average of 53 seconds to complete each question (more on time in the next tip). Finding the correct information quickly is important, as it also takes time to accurately interpret the text and determine an answer. The following tips will help you find the necessary information efficiently when you are searching through the text.

a. **Helpers for your Search**

When searching for answers, you want to look for words and punctuation that will catch your eye quickly. Some things are particularly easy to spot: capitalized proper nouns, unusual words, very long words, quotation marks, numbers, and dates.

If possible, tailor your searches to looking for easily noticed words. For example, if a question asks about stadiums in Norway, you would search for the word *Norway* (capitalized proper noun), not the word *stadium*. Or if the answer choices are all dates (1942, August 30, etc.) from the text, look for these before you look for anything in the question. Finding the dates will be faster than skimming for a few words from the question.

b. **Look for Ideas, not just Words**

While the last tip gave some pointers about which words to look for, finding certain words will not work every time. Sometimes the wording in the question does not match up 100% to the wording in the passage. **The ACT Reading Test is not a word search; it requires thought and interpretation.** As you skim through the text, try to read pieces of information here and there and look for sentences that relate to the question. Keep key words in mind, but be open to anything that seems to match the question's topic. If you just mindlessly search for words, you may never find them. Here is an example to clarify. Read the question first, and then search back into the text for the answer.

The hibernation of the American Black Bear typically begins in October and lasts three to five months. It is not considered a true hibernation, though. Although the species will not venture out of its den but for life-threatening circumstances, the bears are not entirely dormant. Their body temperature stays constant and they are somewhat alert and active. They still are considered hibernators, though, as their heart rate slows considerably, and they do not eat or emit waste. As the weather turns, the Black Bear wanders out of its den and begins to acclimate to an active state.

> Based on the paragraph, does the Black Bear ever leave its place of rest prior to the end of the full hibernation period?
>
> a. Yes, the bear is still active and wanders from its den often
> b. Yes, but only in a dire situation
> c. No, the bear's heart rate has slowed
> d. No, it is asleep and will not wake until completion of the period

The correct answer is B. Answers A and C do match up to sections of the text, but they simply do not answer this question correctly. The paragraph's second sentence says "the species will not venture out of its den but for life-threatening circumstances." Although the wording did not match up perfectly, this says the exact same thing as choice B. Remember that this is not a word search! Even when using the Look-Back Method you have to read, interpret, and understand.

c. Checking First Sentences

When searching for the answer to a question, pay some attention to the first sentence of each paragraph. The first sentence usually introduces the subject of the entire paragraph. Therefore, if the first sentence relates to the question you are working on, there is a good chance your answer is in that paragraph.

If we combine the last three tips (a, b, and c), we form a top-notch strategy for the Look-Back Method: <u>Skim for key words, but also read the first sentence of each paragraph to look for ideas that relate to the question.</u> You may want to tweak this strategy a bit to fit your style, but it is a very good starting point.

d. Pay Attention!!

As you search for answers, you will read a lot of information that doesn't relate to the question you are working on. That doesn't mean it is completely worthless, though! Stay sharp and pay attention to the text. As mentioned earlier, the goal is to begin to understand the passage as you progress through the questions. When you get to later questions, you should start to have an idea of where the answer might be (the beginning, middle, or end of the passage). This tip is easier said than done, but keep it in mind as you practice and you will improve.

e. The Mighty First Paragraph

More answers come from the first paragraph than any other, particularly in the *Science* passages (passages 2 and 4). If any question asks about general, preliminary information, the answer is probably found in or near the first paragraph.

For example, say we have a passage about the migration of a breed of birds. Any of the following facts would probably be found near the beginning of the essay:

- Where the birds originate from and where they go
- The amount of time the journey takes
- The birds' size, species, and physical characteristics

4. *After Finding the Information – Interpreting and Answering*

So you found a key word or a paragraph that matches the ideas in the question. It is smooth sailing from here, right? Unfortunately, that is not true. It is often more difficult to interpret the information than it is to find it in the first place. This is where your reading skills will come into play, so as I've mentioned a few times, becoming a better reader is important even when using the Look-Back Method. Here is a key tip to help you once the answer is within sight:

Read as Much as Necessary

Sometimes the answers to the Reading Test will simply be buried in the text – find the right text and you have the answer. More often, though, you will need to interpret the text and use a little thought to determine the answer. Let's use a 'line-number question' as an initial example. The line numbers are listed on the left, just as they are on the ACT. Since we are using the Look-Back Method, check out the question first, and then come back to the text.

13   As a teenager, I was heavily influenced by my chemistry
     teacher, Doctor Brinkley. I initially had a deserved reputation
15   as a rebel in high school, and while I was not instantly
     transformed to a model student, Doctor Brinkley began
     to instill a new attitude. My meaningless exploits of
     mischievousness tapered as I began to take my studies
     more sincerely. It was no direct action of Doctor
20   Brinkley that changed my behavior, just a general
     feeling that began to form in his presence.

The change in behavior mentioned in lines 19 – 21 can most accurately be described as a shift from:

A. earnest behavior to a more relaxed approach
B. horrible behavior to a more lighthearted approach
C. disobedient behavior to a more serious approach
D. good behavior to more a more rebellious approach

The correct answer is C. If you only read lines 19 – 21 there is no way you could know the answer to this question. **The key is to read and understand the entire thought before you choose an answer.** In this case, you could probably get enough information by beginning reading at line 17. That sentence is a bit difficult to understand, though, so you may even want to start reading from the beginning of the paragraph. The paragraph is only eight short lines and will not take long to get through. After reading the paragraph closely, you see that the narrator started as a mischievous rebel, but then slowly became more of a well-behaved, serious student. Thus, choice C is correct. Choices A and D have the change in behavior backwards. Choice B is too strong – nothing suggested his previous behavior was "horrible." As usual, this question became much easier when the whole thought was taken into account.

5. ***Keeping on Pace***

   The best advantage of the Look-Back Method is that it allows extra time to work on the questions. If you spent no time reading, you have an average of 53 seconds for each question. Here are three tips to help you keep a good pace.

   - It is OK to take a bit longer on the first few questions you complete. While finding the correct answer fast is great, it's also nice (and sometimes necessary) to begin to understand the essay's subject. While working on the first few questions, you may want to read a little extra text to figure out what is happening in the passage. This takes time, but sometimes you need some background knowledge.

   - If a question seems very difficult and you are having no luck finding an answer in the text, it may be smart to give up and take an educated guess. Occasionally students can get too stubborn and waste a few minutes on one question. You can always circle the question and come back later if time permits.

   - Remember the '10 10 10 5 Strategy' (page 63). If you have major troubles finishing all four passages on time, don't get anxious. You can always try to complete three passages strongly and not worry as much about the fourth.

Reading Final Word

Over the last 25 pages I have detailed many different strategies, tips, and tricks designed to maximize your ACT Reading Test score. While these are proven to be effective, it is important to not get bogged down by them all. Try a few that you think may work, and develop a simple style for taking the test. Once you are comfortable with your methods, get relaxed and do not obsess over the tips in this book or any other. The key is to go into the Reading Test with a clear head and confident approach.

And to repeat myself one last time, read as much as possible to prepare for the test. If you become a strong reader this test will be very easy for you.

Next Step: Now that you have finished this section, try the Reading Test from ACT Test form 64E. Time yourself as you complete the test, but don't worry if you go a couple of minutes over; you will get faster with more practice. After taking the test, correct it using the answers and explanations on either page 141 (Reading Method) or 147 (Look-Back Method). A link to ACT Test form 64E is found at ACTPowerPrep.com.

Chapter 4 – Science

Read through this section and then try a practice test. Skim or reread this section after correcting your first practice test, and then try another.

Format and Basic Strategy

The Science Test consists of seven separate passages to be completed in 35 minutes. There are 40 total questions, and you have an average of 53 seconds to complete each one. Let's take a look at the three different types of passages you see on the ACT Science Test. If you have a practice test, flip through and identify the examples of each kind of passage. The passages appear in no particular order on the test.

Data Representations – There are three of these passages per test, with five questions for each of the passages. These passages have one or more graphs or tables and just a little bit of text. These passages mainly test your graph-reading skills.

Research Summaries – There are three of these passages per test, with six questions for each of the passages. These passages focus on an experiment or a couple of different related experiments. They are similar to the Data Representations because they also have graphs or tables, and many questions require basic graph-reading skills. Sometimes these passages also have questions that require logic and reasoning based on the description of the experiment(s).

Conflicting Viewpoint – There is one of these passages per test, and it has seven questions for the passage. This passage is a bit different, as it usually does not have any graphs or tables. The Conflicting Viewpoint passage gives the views of two to four people arguing over a scientific issue (global warming, volcanic eruptions, etc.). It requires more reading skills than the other passages, although plenty of scientific reasoning is used as well. **Many students like to save this passage for last, especially if they have trouble completing the Science Test on time.** It usually is a bit more time consuming than the others, so it can be nice to get all the graph-related passages finished, and then worry about this one. It is easy to spot the Conflicting Viewpoint passage, as it usually is the only one without any tables or graphs.

Note: It is helpful to know the different types of passages, but you don't need to obsess over which kind of passage you are working on. They are all fairly similar and require similar analytical skills. The Conflicting Viewpoint does have some unique features, which I address further on pages 99 – 100.

Before we begin, I should mention that **the ACT Science Test is not a test of your scientific knowledge**. While an A+ in Biology won't hurt, it also won't guarantee a high score. You are aware of this fact if you have taken a practice test. The Science Test is about reasoning and graph interpretation. Occasionally your actual science knowledge is tested, but usually only a couple of times per test. Check out this section and keep practicing to become familiar with the types of questions you will see on test day.

Science Tips, Tricks, and Strategies

1. *Don't Read it to Start*

    When beginning a passage, skip straight to the questions without reading the text. The text is often very scientific and can get you confused before you even begin. Furthermore, usually the text is not all that important. Most of the answers come out of the charts. This tip will save you a significant amount of time and will not hurt your performance at all. **When a question does require use of the text, you can read it as you need it**. More about using the text as you need it appears later in this section.

    Note: If you are aiming for a Science Test score of 30+ and have no issues with finishing the test on time, reading or skimming the text prior to doing the questions may be helpful. Try it each way (reading and not reading) on a practice test and see which you prefer. You can still get a perfect score without reading first, so it purely depends on your preference.

2. *Knowing Question Order*

    Questions get harder as they go <u>within each passage</u>. So Passage One's fifth question will be harder than the first question in Passage One, but about the same difficulty as Passage Two's fifth question. Expect the first couple of questions for each passage to be easy. These questions often only require very basic graph-reading skills. When you move to the last couple of questions for a passage, expect things to get more complicated. These questions may require the use of multiple charts, information from the text, and/or scientific logic. Try some practice passages and you will quickly see this concept in action.

    Note: Occasionally you will see a difficult question in the beginning or an easy question near the end of a passage, but 90% of the time the questions are more or less ranked in order of difficulty.

3. ***Keeping on Pace***

The Science Test is not the most difficult one to finish on time, but many students do have trouble at first. Here are some tips to improve your pace:

- Practice – Practice tests get you comfortable with the style of the exam. Your time will improve as you complete more tests.
- Get your graph-reading techniques down – The more efficient you are at the easy graph-reading questions, the more time you have for the more difficult questions.
- Don't be afraid to skip hard questions – If you are really struggling with a question, take a guess, circle it, and come back to it later if time permits. Don't be too stubborn; you want to **make sure you finish all the easy questions**. Guessing on a difficult question at the end of a passage is not a big deal. Every question, easy or hard, is worth the same amount of points.
- Save the Conflicting Viewpoint for last – As I mentioned before, this passage usually takes the longest, so you have a better chance of staying on pace if you save it for last.

Sample Passage 1 – The following is a Data Representation passage similar to those you see on the ACT Science Test. It will be used to demonstrate graph and table strategy. Skip this page for now, but come back and use the data to answer the questions found on the next few pages.

The flowering plant *elpidus perrenius* was first found in a small area of Prussia in 2005. It is an *invasive species*, meaning that it is not native to the area, and can have adverse effects on other plant life.

Figure 1 shows the ground cover percentages for the *Elpidus P.* and other vegetation measured each June over a five year span. Table 1 shows the heights of five native Prussian species measured in each of the listed years.

Figure 2 shows the *degeneration level* of three Prussian species as determined in June of each year. Degeneration level is a statistic that combines several measures to determine the rate at which a plant species is growing or declining. Table 2 provides a guide to interpreting degeneration levels.

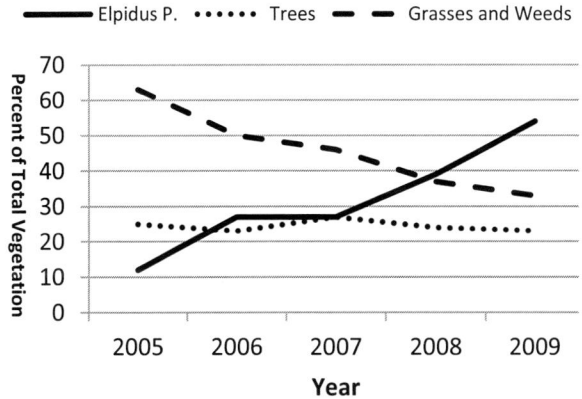

Figure 1

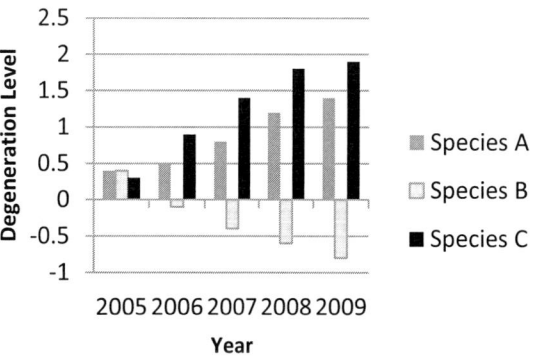

Figure 2

Species	Avg. Plant Height 2005 (in meters)	Avg. Plant Height 2007 (m)	Avg. Plant Height 2009 (m)
A	3.2	2.8	2.2
B	1.1	1.4	1.7
C	.6	.4	.2
D	6.1	6.0	6.1
E	2.3	1.9	1.4

Table 1

Degeneration Level	Effect on Species Population
<-2 to -.5	Strong growth
-.5 to 0	Mild growth
0 to .5	Mild decline
.5 to 2	Strong decline
>2	Threat of extinction from area

Table 2

4. *Go Where They Tell You to Look*

Every passage has several labels and/or headings. Passages start with some text that ACT refers to as either the "passage," the "introductory information," or the "information provided." Then you see other headings and labels such as "Study 1," "Figure 2," etc. Often questions say "From the results of Study 1…" or "Based on information in the passage…" When you see these statements, go right to the mentioned section to find the answer. That is, if it says "Based on Experiment 2…", look under the heading "Experiment 2" to find the answer. 95% of the time the necessary information will be right where they tell you to look. This may seem obvious, but concentrating on the directions can be a big help in finding the correct information, especially on harder questions.

Note: Most Research Summary passages (the ones with six questions) will have several Experiments or Studies labeled (check out page 94 for an example). It is important to know that every Experiment or Study continues until the next one starts. So if under the heading "Study 1" there are two paragraphs and three different graphs before the next heading ("Study 2"), all of that text and those graphs are considered to be part of "Study 1."

5. *Solving Graph Questions – The Power of Axes and other Labels*

The key to being a great reader of graphs, tables, and other charts is one word: AXES! (Axes are the sides of a graph that label the information presented). Maybe one word is a little too simple, because we also need table headings, keys, and all sorts of other labels. The graphs on the ACT Science Test come from professional experiments and real-world research. They will be perfectly labeled so readers can understand the data presented.

When you work on any graph-related question, the simplest way to find the answer is to match up the information in the question to an axis (or key, heading, etc.) of one of the charts in the passage. From there you can plot points, find values, or move on to the next step of the problem. Let's see a couple of examples to clarify.

> According to Figure 1, the greatest percent of vegetation for grasses and weeds over the 5 year span was closest to which of the following?
>
> A. 35%
> B. 55%
> C. 65%
> D. 75%

The correct answer is C. This is a typical basic graph question. You simply go to Figure 1 and match up information in the question to the labels of the graph. Grasses and weeds are labeled as the dashed line, the Y (vertical) axis gives percent of vegetation, and the X (horizontal) axis gives the years. Over those five years, the highest percent of vegetation value for grasses and weeds is in 2005, when the value appears to be about 65%.

> In 2008, Species E's average plant height was most likely closest to which of the following?
>
> A. 2.0 m
> B. 1.6 m
> C. 1.3 m
> D. 1.1 m

The correct answer is B. In this question, they do not tell us directly which chart to look at. So, we need to determine this by finding the chart that has axes or headings that match up with information in the question. The only place we see Species E and plant height is in Table 1, so that is a logical place to begin. On the top row of the table, we see plant height values for 2007 and 2009, but not 2008. Thus, we have to estimate 2008's value. Since Species E's height was 1.9 meters in 2007, and 1.4 meters in 2009, it is logical that the height in 2008 would be somewhere between those values.

*Note: Many students tend to overthink questions like the one above, but **the Science Test is easier than it looks! Questions involve basic logic, not deep scientific thought. If an answer seems to make sense, go with it. If you are thinking about complicated scientific concepts, you probably missed a much easier way to solve the problem.***

6. ***Breaking Down the Question***

ACT Science Test questions can appear long and complicated. Often, though, they are much easier than they look. Try to break down the questions and find the truly important information you need to get started. Let's see some examples of breaking down the question:

Degeneration levels between .5 and 1.0 are known as the *red levels*, as further damage often causes irreversible effects for certain species. Which combination of species and year is in the *red levels?*

A. Species A in 2008
B. Species C in 2008
C. Species B in 2005
D. Species C in 2006

The correct answer is D. This is an elementary example of breaking down the question. The question asks about "red levels," but the only important, usable information was that red levels equal degeneration levels between .5 and 1. Degeneration levels appear on the Y axis of Figure 2. Forget about all the "red level" stuff and simply look for the value between .5 and 1.

In June of 2010, three scientists formed hypotheses before computing the 2010 degeneration levels. Scientist 1 claimed Species B's population would experience strong growth. Scientist 2 claimed Species B would experience mild growth. Scientist 3 claimed Species B would have a mild decline. Based on Figure 2 and Table 2, who is most likely correct?

A. Scientist 1
B. Scientist 2
C. Scientist 3
D. None of the above

The correct answer is A. Again, this question looks harder than it is. Let's break it down to the important information.

- We are dealing with Figure 2 and Table 2
- We need the extent of growth for Species B in the year 2010
- We eventually need to pick the correct scientist, but let's save that for later

We find Species B in Figure 2. The year we need is 2010, which is not on this graph. We can make an educated guess about 2010, though, as we have data for the five previous years. Looking at the pattern, it appears that the degeneration level for Species B will be around -1 in 2010.

Next we move to Table 2 so we can interpret the information and find the extent of growth. According to the table, a degeneration level of -1 would register as strong growth. Looking back to the question, we see that Scientist 1 is the person with the correct hypothesis.

Note: Notice how I took this question one step at a time. **Science Test questions become much simpler if you complete one task before moving on to the next.** *You will often find each individual step in the process is fairly straightforward. Conversely, it is easy to get lost or confused when trying to process two or three pieces of information at once.*

Note: Some students may have guessed on the previous answer without consulting Table 2. However, ACT would never expect you to know what value is "strong growth," "weak decline," etc. ACT expects you to know about basic science, but not about unusual statistics like "degeneration levels." **The information you need will be there somewhere.**

A Word about Extra Information – Look back to the last question and note how it started with, "In June…" This is an example of 'extra information.' The graphs don't have any information about certain months; they only have labels for whole years. Sometimes Science Test questions give a bit of extra information that is not needed to answer the question. Therefore, if you come to a well-thought-out answer that does not incorporate a small piece of information, go with it anyway. If your answer seems shaky, or like something is missing, see if it's possible to use the extra data. There is no way to know which information is unnecessary, but with practice it becomes easy to ignore unneeded facts.

Note: Often the extra bit of information is right in the beginning of the question, as in the previous example. Furthermore, usually this extra information is just repeating something from the text. For the previous example, look at the text above Figure 2. It says that the degeneration levels were determined in June. The question just repeated this.

Note: Overall, don't worry too much about extra information. It usually is fairly easy to recognize when something is unnecessary to the question, especially after a couple of practice tests.

7. *Questions Involving Multiple Graphs*

As you move to more difficult questions, you will run into questions involving multiple graphs. These can seem somewhat overwhelming, but, if approached correctly, they are not too bad. With these questions it is extra important to take things one step at a time. Find the first piece of information, process it, and then move forward. If you find it helpful, write notes or circle information as you go.

Often the hardest part of 'multiple graph questions' is making comparisons between two different graphs. Again, the key to success is using the axes and labels. When two graphs share a common axis or label, you can make comparisons between the two. Let's see an example to clarify:

> Species C is *Toshin Ivy*, a type of wild grass found in Prussia. Scientists hypothesized that at the same time *Toshin Ivy* first entered into a period of strong decline, the *Elpidus Perrenius* would become the dominant plant type in terms of percent of vegetation. Is this hypothesis correct?
>
> A. Yes, *Elpidus P.* became the most common type of vegetation in 2008
> B. Yes, *Elpidus P.* surpasses trees in percent of vegetation
> C. No, *Toshin Ivy* does not enter into a period of strong decline
> D. No, grasses and weeds are the most common type of vegetation in 2006

The correct answer is D. Let's solve this question step by step. Note that your method to solving may not match up perfectly to mine. On harder questions like this one, there is not one definite way to solve the problem. The important thing is to take things one step at a time.

- To begin, let's cut out the fluff and simplify the question. It is basically asking, 'When Species C first enters into a period of strong decline, does *Elpidus P.* have the highest percent of vegetation?'
- To start, we need to find out when Species C first enters a period of strong decline. "Species C" shows up in Table 1 and Figure 2. "Strong decline" is found in Table 2.
- Since Table 2 matches up with Figure 2 (they both have "degeneration level" in them), it looks like we will use those two.
- "Strong decline" equals degeneration values from .5 to 2.0. In Figure 2, Species C first hits a degeneration value of over .5 in 2006. *Notice the connection between charts.*
- Now we can simplify the question again: 'In 2006 does *Elpidus P.* have the highest percent of vegetation?'
- Looking at Figure 1, we find that *Elpidus P.* is the solid line, 2006 is on the X axis, and percent of vegetation is on the Y axis. Reading the graph, we find that in 2006 "grasses and weeds" have the highest percent of vegetation. *Elpidus P.* was not the most common type at this time.
- Now to answer the question – No, when the *Toshin Ivy* entered a period of strong decline (2006), *Elpidus P.* did not become the most common type of vegetation. "Grasses and weeds" were most common at that time.

Don't worry if you found this one confusing, as it is a difficult question. If you don't fully understand it, work through it slowly using my steps and pay special attention to places where I match information from chart to chart. **Carrying information from one chart to another is the key to solving problems that refer to multiple graphs and tables.**

8. *Advanced Science Concepts and Funky Graphs*

The passage we used for the last few examples is fairly easy to understand. We deal with the familiar subject of plant growth, and all the graphs and tables are relatively normal looking. Some ACT passages are straightforward like this, but some are not. Some passages are about advanced and confusing scientific concepts. Some have very odd and unusual looking graphs. Don't be thrown off by this, though! **As long as you use the axes and match information from questions to graphs, you usually don't need to know what the passage is talking about! Remember that this is not a test of your science knowledge: about 75% of the questions can be answered using data in the charts and basic logic.** Still, some questions do require the use of facts from the passage's text and/or more advanced scientific reasoning. Over the next few pages we'll look at ways to efficiently and accurately use logic and the text to answer Science Test questions.

Sample Passage 2 – The following is an example of an Experiment Representation passage. Skip this page for now, but come back and use the data to answer the questions found on the next few pages.

Students investigated several variables effects on the performance of parachutes.

Study 1

Students constructed three parachutes of different shapes out of a nylon material. They attached an equal *payload* (the weight held under the parachute) to each chute with three suspension lines made of string. All three parachutes had a surface area of 2.0 square feet.

In each trial, students dropped the parachute and its payload from a height of 40 feet. The time from release until the payload hit the ground was measured with a stopwatch. The time of the final 10 feet of the fall was measured separately. Students then computed the *terminal velocity* of each parachute in feet per second (ft/sec). In freefall situations, *terminal velocity* refers to the maximum speed an object can reach during a fall. The results were then used to determine the *drag coefficient* of each parachute. The *drag coefficient* is a measure that indicates the level of air resistance provided by an object. All results are listed in the table below.

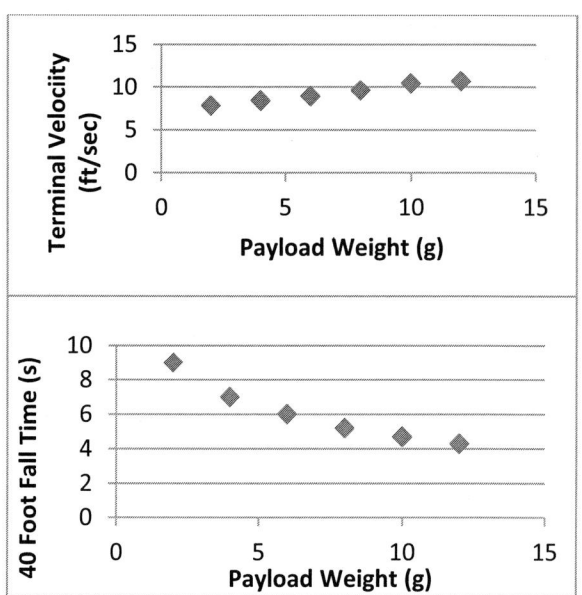

Figure 1

Study 3

Students created a circular parachute as in Study 1, but this time cut a hole with a 3 inch diameter in the center. Five trials identical to Study 1 were performed with the cut parachute and the original full circular parachute. The results were averaged and graphed below.

Shape	40 ft. Time (s)	10 ft. Time (s)	Terminal Velocity (ft/sec)	Drag Coefficient
Circle	6.12	1.12	8.93	1.24
Rectangle	5.32	.98	10.20	1.03
Triangle	5.54	1.04	9.62	1.10

Table 1

Study 2

Students repeated the procedure from Study 1 using the circular parachute. Six trials were performed with different payload weights in each trial. Observations are graphed below.

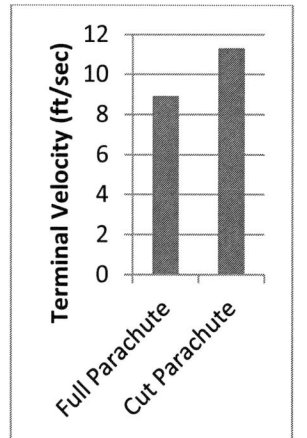 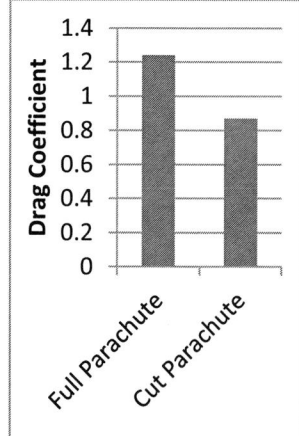

Figure 2

9. ***Moving Beyond Graphs – The Graph to Passage Progression***

The easiest way to complete most questions is by using the tables and graphs. However, on some questions you will need to use information in the text. When you start a question, go to the chart first (go to whichever graph or table is mentioned in the question; if none is mentioned use logic to determine the correct one). If all the information you need can't be found in the chart, then look to the description above the chart. If the information is not there, then look to the passage (the beginning text) to find your answer. This may seem like a long process, but it should only take ten or twenty seconds to get through it. As you practice more and study these tips, this process will become easy to do. You will also learn to recognize problems that look like 'graph questions' and those that seem to be 'text questions.'

Some Things you may Find in the Text

Vocabulary words – If you see a word in a question or graph that seems foreign to you, chances are it is defined somewhere in the passage. ACT rarely expects you to know difficult scientific vocabulary. The defined word will usually be in italics, which makes it easy to find. However, only look for the definition if you truly need it to solve a problem!

Experiment Descriptions and Background Information – The text will tell you the design, purpose, and goals of experiments that appear in the passage. The text also gives you background information for the data presented in graphs and tables. Many 'Research Summary' passages (the ones with six questions) require the use of experiment descriptions to answer a question or two.

Graph and Table Explanations – If you are having trouble interpreting a chart, see if the text above gives you some clues.

10. ***Using the Text***

You are bound to run into roughly six to twelve questions per test that involve the text to some degree (not counting the Conflicting Viewpoint passage, which I address later). Let's get an idea of the basic types of text-based questions you will see on the ACT. Then try the example on the following page (use the data on page 94).

Basic Text Lookup Questions – These questions simply require you to find some information in the text and use it to answer the question. Sometimes you will have to interpret the information using logic and your overall knowledge of the passage; other times you can copy the answer right out of the text.

Text and Graph Questions – So you found some relevant information in a graph, but you are still missing something. There is a good chance the information you need will be in the text somewhere. Often these questions say something like "Based on Figure 1 and the information provided...", although that is not always the case. Remember to take things one step at a time on these.

> In Study 3, students computed a drag coefficient after each trial. They added up all the computed drag coefficients for each parachute, and then divided by what number to determine the value used in Figure 2?
>
> A. 3
> B. 5
> C. 10
> D. There is insufficient information to answer this question

The correct answer is B. The text under "Study 3" says each parachute went through five trials, and the results of these trials were averaged. Using a little math knowledge, we know that adding up the five computed drag coefficients and then dividing that number by five would equal the average.

Note: Occasionally Science Test questions involve some basic math skills. Take your time on these and pay special attention to equations, numbers, and units (i.e. meters, ft/sec, etc.) given in the passage or question.

Note: Although choice D was incorrect on the last example, sometimes "There is insufficient info..." is correct. Don't be afraid to choose it if it's the logical choice.

11. *Don't Shut off Your Brain! The Importance of Common Sense and Logic*

As mentioned earlier, the ACT Science Test does not ask many questions that require scientific knowledge. However, many questions do require logic and common sense. **If an answer just seems to make logical sense, it probably is right. If an answer doesn't make sense, don't choose it. ACT does not purposely try to trick you on the Science Test**. A passage will never say, for example, that an ice cube is hotter than an oven. Graphs and tables will not directly mislead you either. Keep your logic and reasoning working on all types of questions: graph questions, text questions, and any others you run into.

"Most Likely" Questions – On recent tests, more and more questions are focused mainly on logic. Often (not always) these questions have the words "most likely" in them, because the answer cannot be found with certainty in the charts or text. This does not mean the information in the passage should be ignored, though! **Usually you must understand what is happening in the passage in order to reason out the answer.** Let's try two examples of logic-based questions. Note that these questions tend to be difficult, so they are usually found among the last couple of questions for a passage.

Which of the following variables was kept constant in Study 2?

A. Payload weight
B. Triangle parachute surface area
C. Experiment site
D. 10 foot fall time

The correct answer is C. Your first step is to take a look at the graphs and text for Study 2. Next, check out Study 1 to get an idea of the experiment's setup (Study 2 repeats Study 1's procedure). While a definite answer is not found in the passage, **you must understand the design and purpose of the experiment in order to determine the most logical answer**. Once you get some understanding of the passage, check out the answer choices. Choice A is wrong, as the graphs show payload weight changing throughout Study 2. Choice B is wrong, as the triangle parachute was not even involved in Study 2. Choice D is wrong, because it would be impossible to keep 10 foot fall time constant given the experiment's design. The logical answer is choice C. It would make sense to perform all the trials at the same site – this would help you obtain accurate results. Imagine if some trials were done in a wind storm and others in still air. Results would be ruined!

When computing terminal velocity, which fall time did the students most likely use in their calculations?

A. 40 foot, because the parachute was accelerating throughout
B. 40 foot, because the parachute had reached its top speed
C. 10 foot, because the parachute was accelerating throughout
D. 10 foot, because the parachute had reached its top speed

The correct answer is D. Our first step is to find out exactly what terminal velocity is. "Terminal velocity" is the kind of advanced science term that will almost certainly be defined somewhere in the text. Under the heading "Study 1," terminal velocity is defined as "the maximum speed an object can reach during a fall." Thus, while computing terminal velocity, it's logical to use measurements from when the parachute had reached its top speed. This narrows down the answer choices to B and D. Next, looking at the description of Study 1, we see that the parachute was initially dropped from 40 feet. Basic logic says it probably did not reach its top speed instantly. It makes more sense that the top speed had been reached for the last 10 feet of the fall, so the correct answer is D.

12. *'Real Science' Questions*

At least 90% of questions on the Science Test can be completed by interpreting graphs, reading text, and using basic logic. However, roughly one to four times per test your knowledge of actual science concepts is tested. The concepts tested are usually rather simple; ACT does not expect you to know advanced or unusual scientific material. In fact, **if there is a question about a difficult or unusual scientific concept, the answer will be found in the passage somewhere**. ACT only expects you to know basic, introductory facts about Biology, Physics, and Chemistry. You cannot efficiently study for these questions, as they are different every test. Just use a little logic and trust your science knowledge.

A few scientific concepts have come up on multiple tests and are worth reviewing:

1. Dominant / recessive genes and Punnett Squares: This is the most repeated subject for an ACT Science passage. Only a basic, big picture knowledge is necessary. If you need to review this subject, simply search the internet or grab a Biology text book.

2. The PH Scale: A scale from 0 – 14. 0 – 7 are acids, and lower numbers are stronger acids. 7 – 14 are bases, and higher numbers are stronger bases. 7 is neutral.

3. Boiling temperature of water = 100° Celsius. Freezing temperature = 0° Celsius. The freezing and melting temperatures of a substance are always the same.

4. Definitions of kinetic and potential energy. Kinetic energy is the energy of movement – more movement equals more kinetic energy. Potential energy is when something has the potential for movement, like an object high in the air that could fall, or a compressed spring.

5. Definitions of independent variable, dependent variable, and control. Scientists set values for independent variables. The scientist is 'independent' to change them. Dependent variables 'depend' on what happens; basically, they are the results of the experiment. A control is a basic dry run through an experiment that is used for comparison. Again, search the internet if you need a better understanding of these terms. Seeing examples can easily clear up confusion.

13. ***The Conflicting Viewpoint***

As mentioned before, the Conflicting Viewpoint passage (the one with seven questions) is a bit different than the others. It still is based off scientific information, but it requires more interpreting of text than working with graphs. Students are usually taught that this is the hardest passage on the test, but that often is not true. As with the other passages, the information is there, you just need to find and interpret it.

Pinpointing the arguments – Unlike on the other six passages, doing a little bit of reading before moving on to the questions is worth the effort (and I truly mean a *little* bit of reading). There are two goals to the initial review of the Conflicting Viewpoint passage:

1. Determine the passage's subject

2. Get an idea of each person's argument

You can find the passage's subject near the beginning. Usually the first few sentences of the passage plainly state its focus. Don't pay attention to complicated scientific facts; you can always look those up if you need them later. **Just get the basics**.

The Conflicting Viewpoint presents two to four different takes on the issue (check out a practice test and this will become clear). After you find the passage's subject, try to determine the difference in the viewpoints presented. This is easy to do because the viewpoints are usually given in the first sentence or two under each heading. That is, Scientist 1's main viewpoint will be in the first sentence under the heading "Scientist 1." Again, ignore complicated scientific talk; just get the basics.

Note: Finding the subject and each person's viewpoint should only take 20 – 35 seconds.

Note: If you are having trouble understanding the subject or viewpoints, don't worry. Just move on to the questions and start to look up answers.

The Necessary Skills – Conflicting Viewpoint questions are very similar to the other questions on the Science Test, but they also share traits with ACT Reading Test questions. Here's a list of the most important techniques needed for completing these questions, along with the page number where you can find more information on the topic:

Science Based Techniques

- Expect easy questions in the beginning and harder questions at the end. (page 84)
- Break down and simplify the questions if possible. (page 89)
- Take more complicated questions one step at a time. (pages 90 – 92)
- Always use common sense and basic logic. (page 96)

Reading Based Techniques

- Mine through the text to find the information that relates to the question. (pages 79 – 81)
- Actually interpret the text if you can. Don't just mindlessly look for certain words. (pages 76, 81 – 82)

Further notes on Conflicting Viewpoint questions

- Many of the questions relate directly to the main arguments of the 'Scientists' or 'Students' (the viewpoints you found in the beginning). **Always keep the primary viewpoints in mind while completing the questions.**
- There is usually one 'real science question' (page 98) on each Conflicting Viewpoint passage. Other than that, you will simply be looking up answers (and using a little common sense and logic).
- As always, practice will make you more comfortable with this passage.

Next Step: Now that you have made it through this chapter, try the Science Test from ACT form 64E. After you complete the test, review the answers and explanations found on page 153 of this book (learn from your mistakes!). ACT form 64E can be downloaded at ACTPowerPrep.com

Chapter 5 – Writing

After completing the four main sections of the ACT, you may also take the optional ACT Writing Test. Many colleges require this test and, unless you see writing as a major weakness, it is probably to your advantage to give it a try. **Taking the Writing Test does not affect your composite (overall) score at all.** If you choose to take Writing, you will receive two extra scores. You will be given a score on a 2 – 12 scale for the Writing Test, and you will be given a Writing / English score, which combines your Writing and English scores on a 1 – 36 scale. Your subtest scores (including English) and composite score are not changed by taking the Writing Test.

You probably have plenty of practice writing essays for your English and Social Studies classes, but writing under timed conditions is quite different. Pick a couple of topics and write at least two timed practice essays before you take the real test. If possible, get your English teacher to look over your essays and offer advice. Writing topics from previous ACT Tests can be found with a simple online search.

Format

The Writing Test gives you 30 minutes to plan and write an essay. The topic or "prompt" is chosen by ACT and connects to some issue relevant to a high school student. You will not know the prompt until the test begins. Each prompt gives two options, for example, "Should high school be in session all year, or should a summer break be maintained?" It is your job to take a position on the issue and support your argument logically. ACT grades you on both how well you write and how well you support your position.

This section contains several tricks and tips that all pertain to one goal: writing a well-constructed ACT essay. I do not focus on general writing skills because you learn those in English class. I begin this section with a rundown of the exact standards ACT graders use when they score your essay. The tips and tricks follow.

Grading Standards and Basic Strategy

Your essay will be given a score of 1 – 6 by two separate graders. Their grades are combined to give you an overall score of 2 – 12. The following are the nine things you must do to get a top score on the ACT Writing Test. These are based on the exact standards ACT graders use when scoring your essay.

1. *Understand the Prompt*

    Your essay should directly address the prompt and stay focused on the topic. All your arguments should directly relate to the prompt. Top-scoring essays show a clear understanding of the issue and encourage further intelligent discussion about it.

2. *Take a Position on the Issue*

    Each prompt gives two sides to an issue. Make sure you pick one side and stick with it for the whole essay. Be as persuasive as possible in supporting your position on the issue. *Tip 2* gives a guideline for which side of the issue to pick.

3. *Fully Develop your Ideas*

    Concentrate on a few main points and go into detail on them in your body paragraphs. Fully support your main ideas with several reasons and examples. Don't just write down a long list of undeveloped arguments. See *Tip 4* for more on this.

4. *Organize and Sequence your Ideas*

    Keep a basic organization pattern. Start with an introductory paragraph, then move on to the body paragraphs, and then finish with a concluding paragraph. Try to place all your main arguments in a logical order that flows naturally. Figure out the sequencing of your essay before you start writing it (see *Tip 1*).

5. *Have a Clear Introduction and Conclusion*

    An introduction and a conclusion are necessary parts of your ACT essay. See *Tip 3* and *Tip 6* for extended sections on introductions and conclusions.

6. *Evaluate Complications and Respond to Counterarguments*

　　You should anticipate some of the arguments for the other side of the issue (*counterarguments*) and respond to them briefly in your essay. This is elaborated on in *Tip 5*.

7. *Use Transitions*

　　Try to move from one idea to another in a natural, logical way. An essay with no transitions appears choppy and will not earn a very high score. You want to begin thinking about transitions while initially planning your essay (see *Tip 1*).

8. *Vary Sentence Structure and Use Good Vocabulary*

　　This really comes down to your overall writing ability. Strong use of vocabulary looks great to ACT graders, but make sure the word fits 100%. Misuse of vocabulary will end up hurting your score.

9. *Avoid Errors*

　　Of course, no one wants to make mistakes in spelling or grammar, but it does happen. The main goal is to make sure the errors do not distract the reader from making sense of your essay. If you have time, go back and check for errors when you finish your essay.

Writing Tips, Tricks, and Strategies

1. *Plan It Out!!!*

    ACT puts an emphasis on having a well-organized and logically sequenced essay. This is very difficult to accomplish if you do not take some time to plan. Your ACT booklet gives you a page to plan your work and you definitely should take advantage of it. I recommend using your first two to five minutes working solely on idea generation and general organization. Once you come up with your arguments, examples, reasons, etc. you will be able to write your essay fairly quickly, and will easily make up for the few minutes of preparation. Everyone's writing style is different, but regardless you want to accomplish at least three things during the planning stage.

    a. Come up with your basic arguments and make sure you can support them; find at least one response to the main counterargument (argument for the other point of view).
    b. Begin to develop your introduction and general thesis statement (one sentence that sums up your entire essay).
    c. Begin to plan the sequence of ideas in your essay. Think of how you will be able to effectively transition from one idea to another.

    Once you have accomplished these three tasks, you will be ready to write a strong essay. Some of the upcoming tips elaborate on these ideas.

2. *Picking the Correct Side*

    Besides testing your general writing skills, this section tests your ability to support an argument. So, **choose the side of the argument that you can support the best**. If the question asks "Should school be in session all year or should a summer break be maintained?" you may want to pick "school all year" even if the thought of it makes you cringe. If your best support for the summer break would be "I like to sit on the couch and watch baseball all day," this would not be the best choice. Don't worry; an ACT grader will not go tell your friends that you want to be in school all year.

    Note: You can also choose a different solution to the issue. For example, you could argue that the summer break should only be one month, or that intensive summer reading programs should be required. Just make sure you have good reasons, details, and examples to support your argument. **The goal is to be as persuasive as possible!**

3. ***Setting the Tone: Good Introductory Paragraphs***

Writing a great introductory paragraph is a difficult task, especially under timed conditions. For this reason, ACT graders do not expect an ultra-creative introduction. They mainly want you to accomplish a few basic tasks, which I list under the *Musts* heading below. If you can effectively complete these four *Musts*, you will be on pace for a solid score of 8 to 10, and an 11 or 12 will certainly be possible. Now, if inspiration strikes, a creative introductory paragraph can help you earn an extra point and/or put you on pace for a score of 11 or 12. I list some ideas for unique introductory paragraphs under the *Bonus: Creative Openers* section on the next page.

Musts:

a. <u>Make your introduction at least three sentences.</u> If it is less you probably will lose a point. A solid four to seven sentence introduction will get your essay started well. However, you don't want to repeat yourself or lose track of your arguments. **Stay focused on the issue and introduce the arguments for your side.**

b. <u>Speak to the topic of the essay and clearly present your view on the issue.</u> You may want to come right out with your view in the first sentence. Alternatively, you can wait a couple of sentences if you are using some sort of creative opening. Either way, your opinion on the issue should be distinctly stated in the first paragraph. In general, it is safer to present your view early in the introductory paragraph than near the end of it.

c. <u>Give some reference to the points you will make in your essay.</u> Try not to give away all your best reasons, though. You want to speak generally in the introduction and then get into the specific details of your main points later in the essay. As another tactic, you can give one example or detail that speaks to all of your main points. Referencing your arguments makes for an easy, but effective way to fill out your introductory paragraph.

d. <u>Have one clear thesis statement.</u> This sentence clearly presents your view on the essay. It should also either hint at your supporting arguments or come right out with them. If you are having trouble devising a thesis, you can simply end the paragraph with an all-encompassing thesis sentence like this one:

> School should be extended to the summer months to keep teenagers out of trouble, prepare them better for college, and allow them more time to pursue non-required classes.

This kind of sentence does a good job of introducing your arguments and establishing your position, although something more creative will help slightly if you are shooting for a score of 10 or higher

Bonus: Creative openers (Make sure you still follow all the *Musts*; they are needed whether you use a creative opener or not!)

a. <u>Tell an Anecdote (short story).</u> Take your best example and relate it to the overall topic of your essay. Try to connect your story to as many of your arguments as possible. The story does not have to be 100% true, so meld it to fit your main points. Once you finish the anecdote, comment on it for a sentence or two, or go right into a thesis statement that plainly states your position and main arguments. Just don't ramble; starting with a long, slow-moving story will hurt your score.

b. <u>Squash a significant counterargument.</u> When skillfully done, this can make for an attention-grabbing start to an essay. Here is an example:

> Requiring children to stay in school during the summer seems to be an obvious way to improve young students' intellects and keep them focused on their studies. But in a world of diminishing attention spans, mandatory summer school would end up having the opposite effect….

You may go on to make the point that students would be too distracted and more dropouts would result. You still could tie in other unrelated points (like the need for summer jobs), especially if you use some smooth transitions.

c. <u>Surprise the reader.</u> Say something bold. Maybe start with an exclamation. Get creative. ACT readers read thousands of similar essays and appreciate some pizzazz. With that said, don't force it. A basic opening stating your view on the issue is superior to something creative that does not make sense and/or fit the topic. Here is an example of a surprising opening sentence:

> High school students are lazy. Their future jobs will not have summer breaks. Why should they get used to it as they prepare for adulthood?

The preceding sentence also demonstrates the tactic of <u>starting with a rhetorical question</u> (a question not intended to be answered). Rhetorical questions can be overused, so be careful, but sometimes they are a useful way to get your reader's attention.

d. <u>Get historical.</u> If you are familiar with the subject, you may be able to comment on the past and use it to lead into your future recommendations on the issue. Example:

> Summer breaks started because farm children were expected to help their parents over the summer months...

Note: Be careful with creative openers – misusing them will hurt your score. Basic, traditional introductory paragraphs can still earn high scores. Don't force it!

4. ***Body Paragraphs: Supporting your Arguments***

ACT graders reward fully-developed arguments with the highest scores. You will have a tough time elaborating on your points if you choose five different arguments to try and support. **I recommend only picking two or three main ideas and spending an entire paragraph explaining each one.** If you have five great arguments, try to combine them or twist them slightly so you can use one to support another.

The best arguments are those that you can support with strong reasons, examples, and details. While being creative certainly helps, even the most obvious arguments will earn high scores if you support them well. Each argument should have roughly two to four verifying reasons or examples, although this is not an exact science. Here is an example of prewriting (planning) a supporting argument and the paragraph that results:

> *(Prewriting) Reason for no school in the summer: Many students hold summer jobs*
> - *Students can save money to pay for college*
> - *You begin to learn about the working world*
> - *My job at the grocery store taught me responsibility*

> The summer break gives students the opportunity to take on jobs which are more beneficial to them than an extra three months of school. With the rising costs of college and our country's economic state, many students rely on summer occupations to save money for their upcoming college years. In addition, summer jobs teach students valuable lessons in responsibility that they will use as they move on to the 'real world.' Showing up late to school means a tardy slip or possibly an hour of detention; showing up late to your job could result in getting fired. Personally, my job at the local grocery store has helped greatly in my transition from a dependent adolescent to a self-sufficient man. The financial and personal gains I have made in my summer work are far more valuable than an extra three months of classes.

Notice how I stick to one main point for the entire paragraph and stay on track with the supporting details. I transition between reasons and examples and do not get stuck repeating myself. Furthermore, I hint at some defense against counterarguments by comparing the consequences of being late to school and being late to work (the counterargument being that school teaches responsibility just as well as a job). This paragraph, along with an introduction, conclusion, and one or two other supporting paragraphs, would make for a very strong essay.

Here's another quick tip that I mentioned briefly earlier:

Not everything you say needs to be 100% true: OK, I confess, I never worked at a grocery store. The ACT grader will not do a background check, though! In addition, I just assumed that college costs are rising; I really don't know the exact trends of the last few years. This is not to say that you should lie just for the sake of lying. Nor should you make up far-fetched facts or stories that are unnecessary, distracting, and/or suspicious. But the occasional presumed fact or borrowed story will not get you into trouble if appropriately placed.

5. **Smashing Counterarguments**

   Graders like to see that you acknowledge the views of others by responding to counterarguments. At the same time, you do not want to make this a central part of your essay. Most of your essay should be dedicated to reinforcing your own ideas. Treat responses to counterarguments as another method to support your main points. Just be careful to make sure everything still transitions smoothly. Don't force it; a response to a counterargument can fit nearly anywhere in your essay. Go back a page and check out the sample paragraph under *Tip 4*. Notice how the response to the counterargument is mixed in with other details.

   Note: When you are responding to counterarguments, either briefly explain why the other side's arguments are incorrect, or simply say why your arguments are more important than theirs. Furthermore, try to attack the other side's most obvious arguments. It is very persuasive if you can explain the flaws or relative unimportance of their biggest argument.

6. **Ending strongly: The Conclusion**

   The conclusion is your last chance to impress the reader. A good one can make up for an otherwise average essay. There are several aspects common to good conclusions, and a few things that should be avoided. Also, there are a few standard methods to constructing conclusions. They are all listed on the next two pages.

Good conclusions contain:

a. <u>A rephrasing of your thesis statement.</u> This will reinforce your views and show the true purpose of your essay. However, do not give a word-for-word reproduction of the thesis used in your introduction. The rephrased thesis sentence can be placed anywhere in the conclusion.

b. <u>At least three sentences.</u> Short conclusions make it look like you ran out of thoughtful things to say. Graders will be left with a bad final impression

c. <u>A sense of completeness.</u> Don't leave questions unanswered.

Avoid these in your conclusion:

a. <u>Starting with "In conclusion…" or "To summarize…"</u>

b. <u>Introducing new topics.</u> This is why you have body paragraphs. If you just came up with a great idea, sorry, it's probably too late.

c. <u>Making your point for the first time.</u> Sometimes students like to leave an air of mystery around their main points throughout the essay, and then drill them in during the final paragraph. While that can work in certain papers, the ACT essay is meant to be persuasive throughout; this approach will not work here.

Conclusion strategies (use one or a couple of these together to end strongly):

a. <u>Summarize and synthesize.</u> Summarizing your main arguments is a classic way to end a paper. However, simply repeating your earlier arguments will make for a boring conclusion. **Try to bring your main points together (synthesize) to make some general statements on the issue.** In addition, try to use different language and sentence structure when summarizing past points.

b. <u>Make a recommendation for further action.</u> Recommendations are a great way to end a paper, although sometimes they are not practical given the topic. Use wisely. Here is an example of a good use of recommendations, and then one that is a bit over the top:

> Good use: As we approach another school year, we should ask our educators, why are our country's young minds falling behind the rest of the world during a lazy summer break?

Bad use: We should march to our local congressmen and tell them to mandate the summer break for the sake of our young students.

c. <u>Give a tangible solution.</u> **Make a plea for a certain course of action. Just make sure it fits with the rest of your essay and isn't coming out of nowhere. In fact, you probably want to hint at this solution during the introduction and body paragraphs. Your conclusion should not surprise the reader at all. Here's an example of a creative, tangible solution:**

While a summer break is best for our young students, mandatory usage of summer reading programs would force students to keep their minds active during this time off.

d. <u>Reference your anecdote from the introduction.</u> **You are certain to wow readers if you can start a story in the introduction, go on to make your points, and then finish the story or provide commentary on it in your conclusion. This is easier said than done, but it is doable if you plan it out during your prewriting time.**

e. <u>Suggest the importance of your view.</u> **By taking your recommendation, what is going to happen? How is this going to change things? Why is this important?** Answering any of these questions will add a lot of meaning to your essay. You can also take a passive approach to using this strategy. Sometimes you can suggest the importance of your view just by 'synthesizing' your main arguments (instead of directly answering the above questions). Either way can be effective.

Note: Some of these conclusion strategies are designed for advanced writers looking for a top score. If you do not see writing as a strength for you, keep things simple and don't try to do too much. A simple summary of your main points can still earn a good score.

7. ***The Final Edit***

Once your introduction, body, and conclusion are complete, read over your essay if you have extra time. Correct errors, throw in some better vocabulary words, and make sure your message is clear during this review time. You probably do not have time to make any significant changes to your essay, so be confident and just tidy up your work.

8. ***Bonus Writing Skills Tip: Being Persuasive***

Essay graders read hundreds of similar essays. The best way to stand out is by making strong, persuasive points. Let's look at some ways to do this.

For the examples we will use the following topic: *Should high school students be required to maintain a "C" average in order to have a driver's license?*

- <u>*Cut down on generic sentences*</u> – Many students have a habit of repeating the same general, big-picture ideas in their ACT Writing essays. They forget to support these ideas with specific reasons and examples. Let's look at an example of 'generic writing':

    > Teenagers who cannot get "C" level grades are not responsible enough to have a driver's license. Driving a car is a serious responsibility. If teens can't even average C's they are not mature enough to drive. There are a lot of programs to get extra help at school. If these people still can't get solid grades, they don't deserve the opportunity to drive…

    Are you yawning yet? The paragraph basically just repeated the idea that students without "C" averages are not responsible enough to drive (three times!). The only time actual support for the argument was given ("there are programs to get help at school"), the reasoning was never developed, and the writer fell back on another generic statement ("they don't deserve the opportunity"). Now let's see part of a paragraph that uses reasons and examples to support the argument:

    > Teenagers who cannot get "C" level grades are not responsible enough to have a driver's license. If students know that a "C" average is all that is required to qualify for a license, it will be their own fault if they do not rise to that level. Academic ability and driving skills may not be directly connected, but reaching a decent GPA demonstrates competency and responsibility. When an inexperienced 16 year old is behind the wheel, those are two qualities anyone on the road certainly hopes the teenager can demonstrate…

    This paragraph actually gives reasons to back up the claim that the students are not responsible enough to drive. It gives specific arguments that would be difficult to disagree with. Furthermore, the main counterargument (that academics and driving ability are unconnected) is shown to be less important than the effect on road safety. This also leads into the next tip:

- <u>*Pretend you are in an argument*</u> – Pretend you are arguing about the "C" average – driver's license issue with friends. What would you say? You would probably give specific examples. You would appeal to your friends' emotions and rational sense. You would shoot down their best arguments. You would try to be as persuasive as possible.

    These are the exact same things you should be doing when supporting your main points. Students get so worried about writing a solid, technically-correct paragraph that they sacrifice actually being persuasive. When you are planning your essay (prewriting), pretend you are in a loud argument about the issue. It will help you to come up with stronger support.

Note: Always choose the side of the issue that you can support better (page 104).

- <u>*Give your sentences life!*</u> – Even good supporting reasons and examples can be written in a boring way. Be specific and relatable in your arguments. Let's see some examples of boring arguments, and then of ways to make them more exciting and persuasive:

Boring argument:	Even good students can be irresponsible or unskilled drivers.
Better version:	As I leave my school, I see plenty of "A" students speeding out of the lot, blasting music, and driving recklessly.
Boring argument:	This policy would encourage students to try harder in school.
Better version:	A normally unmotivated student will study a little harder for his chemistry test if his car privilege is on the line.
Boring argument:	Overall, students with bad grades are more likely to be dangerous drivers.
Better version:	In general, the student who ignores homework and tests is more likely to ignore traffic rules and signals.

    'Boring arguments' should only be used if necessary to get your point across for the first time. Still, always add specific support (like that in the 'better versions') to back up any general statements. If possible, avoid 'boring arguments' altogether.

Note: Becoming a better writer takes work, so just try to improve a little bit with each practice essay. You only have 30 minutes to complete the Writing Test, so your work will never be perfect.

Next Step: Search online for "ACT Test writing prompts." Find a prompt and try a 30 minute timed essay. If you can, have your English teacher or a parent look over your work. In addition, self-correct your work based on the grading guidelines and tips in this book. Make notes on ways you can improve your writing, and then try a second sample essay.

SECTION 2

Answers and Explanations to Official ACT Test 64E

A Link to Test 64E is found at ACTPowerPrep.Com

Log on to ACTPowerPrep.com, find the link to official ACT Test 64E, and print out the test form. Take each section of the test timed. If you don't have three to four hours to take the entire test, it is OK to do one section at a time. You may want to review the tricks, tips, and strategies in this book prior to taking each subtest.

If your test day is approaching, take the test under strict timed conditions (the time limits are on the test form). If you still have some preparation time before test day, you do not have to be as strict about finishing right on time. Either way, try your best to finish within the time constraints.

After you finish, grade your test (a grading scale appears at the end of the test form). Look carefully at the explanations to any questions you missed or were unsure about. The explanations will match up with concepts found earlier in this book. As on every practice test, make an effort to learn from your mistakes.

Note: **This section contains two separate sets of explanations for the Reading Test. The first set is designed for those using the 'Reading Method,' and the second set is for those using the 'Look-Back Method.'** *Also note that the Look-Back Method questions are out of order. This is due to the strategy found on page 78 of this book.*

Test 64E – English Answers and Explanations

Passage I

1. **D**. Keep it simple and to the point. This sentence sounds completely fine with the words omitted; in fact, answers A, B, and C all make the sentence sound a bit clunky and awkward.

2. **H**. Answer exactly what the question asks. We want to suggest a "cautious pace" and "sense of anticipation." Choice H accomplishes both of those goals. Choice J says the word "anticipation," but that does not automatically make it the best answer. This answer gives no mention of the "cautious pace" and thus is incorrect.

3. **A**. Read the entire sentence out loud and pick the answer that sounds correct. Choice A creates a nice, smooth-sounding sentence. Choice C is a common trick – if you do not read from the beginning of the sentence, it can appear that the passage is saying "shapes **reward** the artist." This is incorrect; it is "the view" that **rewards** the artist. Review subject-verb agreement if you missed this one.

4. **G**. Read the entire sentence and see which answer sounds correct. G creates a sentence that flows well. The other options create odd-sounding sentences.

5. **D**. Keep it simple. Whenever "Omit" or "Delete" is an option, look back and determine if the underlined text is new and relevant. In this case, the sentence already said "over many weeks." Thus, answers A, B, and C are not new information – they basically were already said.

6. **H**. This is an example of defining something after a comma (see page 25). The kiln is mentioned, and then there is a comma and a brief explanation of the kiln. You will see sentences like this on nearly every ACT. The problem with choices F and G is that they result in two full sentences with a comma between, which is not grammatically correct (see page 20). J is wrong because it does not get all the information across.

7. **B**. On this question, the information seems to fit well in the passage, so I would lean towards keeping it. Answer B gives a logical reason as to why it should be kept. Answer A is simply not true; this phrase is not about painting. D is wrong because the whole essay is full of details, and this description is not out of place. C is decent, but given the context (nearby sentences) this detail does not seem unimportant to the essay. See page 19 for more on this type of question. Note that "preceding sentence" means the sentence just before the boxed number.

8. **F**. Keep it simple. The sentence already said she was crouching. G, H, and J basically repeat that.

9. **B**. Commas are just pauses in speech. The natural pauses in this sentence occur as written in answer B. This is also an example in which two commas are put around an extra piece of information that could be taken out of the sentence (see page 20). Answer C is incorrect because we need full sentences on either side of a semicolon, which does not happen here (see page 21).

10. **F.** Answer exactly what the question asks. We want to "indicate that... the fire is extremely intense." Although a couple of these answers are OK, F is the best in that the image of the "inferno roar(ing)" really gets the intensity across. Answer J tries to trick you by actually saying the word "intense," but it still doesn't get the extreme intensity across quite as well as F.

11. **D.** "Time or again" does not sound right at all. As with all 'NOT acceptable questions,' look at every single one of the options and don't rush to a decision. While choice C may sound a little odd, D is definitely the worst of the four.

12. **F.** This question illustrates why you should pay some attention to the content you are reading. While choice F is grammatically correct, the passage is saying that the sparks are **going out** of the chimney, not that they are shooting **at** the chimney. G, H, and J all have the correct meaning and grammar.

13. **C.** Another example of answering exactly what is asked. We want "specific detail" and to "maintain the style and tone of the essay." Choices A and B are short on detail, so they do not work. D has plenty of detail, but it doesn't match the direct writing style we have seen throughout this essay. C gets to the point while still adding the detail about the fire reaching 1000 degrees. It is the best answer.

14. **J.** First of all, J just sounds the best when you read each option as part of the whole sentence. Choice G sounds awkward, and also creates two whole sentences with a comma between (see page 20). Choice H sounds completely wrong. Choice F never establishes what exactly has died down. We cannot simply infer that they are talking about the fire (see page 24).

15. **A.** Choice A is the simplest answer and it creates the most readable sentence. Notice that choices B and C use the word "which." Answers that use the word *which* are wrong at least 90% of the time. Don't choose *which* unless you are sure it is correct.

Passage II

16. **J.** Keep it simple and don't repeat information. The sentence already said it was a business trip.

17. **C.** Read each choice out loud. C clearly does not work. The others are all OK.

18. **F.** There is no pause in this sentence, thus no comma is needed. Think about how you would say this sentence out loud. While H may look right, you want to trust how it sounds, not how it looks.

19. **B.** First read the entire sentence as written in the passage, and then read it as written in the question. This will help you pinpoint the difference. Choices C and D do not fit with the content of the story; we would be inferring information that just isn't there (don't infer things that aren't plainly said!). B fits with her expecting an item, but then unexpectedly being led outside. Furthermore, if we skim ahead to the next paragraph, we find the gift is actually a tortoise. This confirms that B makes sense.

20. **F.** In *of vs. have* situations such as this one, *have* is always the correct choice. Phrases like *must of, could of, would of,* etc. are always incorrect.

21. **C**. Try all four options. Notice how A, B, and D all function basically the same way; this is your first sign that C is the odd one out here. Furthermore, C is not acceptable because it creates two full sentences with a comma between, which is grammatically incorrect.

22. **F**. Take your time on 'order questions' like this one, as there always is a clear reason for where the sentence should be located (see page 18). In sentence two, the author begins using the name Rosie. It would make sense to introduce Rosie before using her name casually, so F is the best choice.

23. **B**. This is a classic double comma situation. The statement "it turns out" is an extra phrase that has been thrown into the sentence. It could easily be removed, and the sentence would still be grammatically correct. For more on this see page 20. If you chose answer A, look over the grammar of colons on page 21.

24. **H**. H has the most awkward wording of the four choices, so it is the unacceptable option. Furthermore, notice that F and G are identical other than a small difference in word choice. How could only one of those answers be acceptable? When answers are that similar, neither one of them will be the correct choice.

25. **B**. We must look for clues in the text to determine the tense of this sentence. Because the girl's parents had already "agreed" (past tense), we know that she "had checked" with them in the past.

26. Given that this question deals with information that is presented later in the paragraph, we will revisit this after # 29.

27. **D**. Choices A and B are far too wordy. C is unclear and a little too informal. Choice D is the most simple, clear, and readable option.

28. **F**. Answer exactly what the question asks – F is definitely the most "specific" and "precise" choice.

29. **A**. There is possession, as the backyards do belong to the parents. Thus, we need an apostrophe. She is talking about more than one parent (it was plural already), so the *s'* is the correct choice. For more on this see page 23.

26 (revisited). **G**. The paragraph describes what Rosie eats and how the narrator can keep the tortoise safe. G is the best introduction to this information.

30. **G**. Read the entire sentence – G simply sounds better than the other options.

Passage III

31. **B**. The farm belongs to the family. The passage is talking about just one family (it was not plural already). Thus, *'s* is correct (see page 23).

32. **F.** First of all, this answer creates a sentence that just does not sound right. Second, if we used F, the text would have to indicate who was limiting his access to education directly after the comma. See page 24 for a full explanation of this important concept.

33. **B.** Substitute the word *she* for the underlined word – notice that the phrase "she, after…, bought some land…" sounds perfectly correct. This proves that "who" is the best answer (see page 22 to learn this trick). Choice C is incorrect because we do not use "which" to refer to people. D is incorrect because it creates a fragmented sentence that is hard to understand.

34. **J.** Although this explanation is somewhat helpful, the essay focuses on Banneker's life and this statement seems out of place and unnecessary. On questions like this one it helps to read ahead a bit to see where the paragraph is going. If the next few sentences focused on the rights of indentured servants, then F or G would probably be correct.

35. **C.** While both A and D sound choppy, they still are grammatically correct (also remember that a semicolon functions the same way as a period, so these answers are basically identical). Choice C contains two complete sentences strung together and is grammatically incorrect.

36. **H.** Take an extra moment when you are given long answer choices such as these. Choice H has a logical progression of words and sounds smooth. The others do not get the ideas in the correct order and sound awkward.

37. **C.** See page 25. The possessive form of *it* is always *its*.

38. **H.** Choices F, G, and H all work grammatically, so we need to figure out the tense based on nearby sentences. Looking back in this paragraph, we see that the clock was made in the 1700s. H (past tense) is the only answer that makes sense.

39. **D**. Keep it simple. Choices A, B, and C add extra words that are completely unnecessary.

40. **F.** First of all, we have two full sentences, so only F and G have the correct punctuation. Next we must reread the previous sentence to find which of these 'transition words' makes sense in context. "Therefore" means *as a result*; it would not be a logical way to connect these two unrelated thoughts. "In addition" does work as a logical transition. See page 16 for more on this kind of question.

41. **A.** Choices B, C, and D are simply not true. The bit about learning these instruments has no link to the last paragraph. It is not humorous. And finally, it is not an "extensive digression." Choice A is true. The fact that Banneker taught himself flute and violin supports that he enjoyed learning. We would lose that if the last part of the sentence was deleted.

42. **G.** It is difficult to tell exactly what "them" or "those" refers to. Choice G is much clearer. <u>If you have the choice of choosing between a pronoun and the actual noun, go with the noun.</u>

43. **D.** The sentence already says "annual tables." Choices A, B, and C add words that mean the same

thing as "annual." Never add words unless they present new and important information (see page 11).

44. **J**. Although all of these answers are decent, J best sums up the main ideas of the essay as a whole. The other choices focus too heavily on smaller sections of the essay. On questions like this one it can be helpful to skim back over the passage to remind yourself of its main points.

45. **A**. When we take some time and look closely at the essay, we find that the years progress from 1753 in paragraph 3, to 1759 in paragraph 4, to 1788 here. Thus, chronologically it fits as the fifth paragraph.

Passage IV

46. **J**. Keep it simple. The sentence already says kayaks are used in "wilderness areas"; choices F, G, and H are not adding any new information. "Wilderness areas" are always wild, remote, and uncivilized.

47. **C**. Choices A, B, and C all make grammatically correct sentences, so we need to read back to the last sentence to determine the correct pronoun. "They" is correct because it is referring back to the word "kayaks," which is plural.

48. **G**. This paragraph (and the essay in general) focuses on kayaks, so it would be helpful to have this description of how a kayak looks. The sentence doesn't mention different types of kayaks, so choice F is incorrect. Again, note that "preceding sentence" means the one before the numbered box.

49. **C**. Choices A, B, and D add unnecessary stops to a sentence that flows well without any pauses. Resist the tendency overuse commas and other punctuation! (see page 13)

50. **J**. Read the entire sentence from "The two..." all the way to the period. Choice J simply sounds the best. Grammatically, "larger" is better than "largest" because we are only comparing two kayaks. "-est" is used when comparing three or more things.

51. **C**. This is a case where "the tumultuous… rivers" is extra information added to the sentence. We could remove this statement and the sentence would still work. In this case, commas are placed on either side of the extra information. Furthermore, choices A and D sound awkward, as they ignore necessary pauses in speech. Choice B breaks the rule about semicolons (page 21).

52. **J**. While every one of these options works grammatically, only J makes sense in context. The previous sentence said that the boats do not capsize (tip over) easily. This sentence says that the kayakers wear safety gear. "Nevertheless" is the only logical transition between these somewhat conflicting ideas. If you struggled with this, check out page 16 for more on this kind of question.

53. **D**. This question is very similar to the last (#52). "Yet" is the only option that does not logically connect the two sentences. Again, review page 16 if you missed this one.

54. **F**. Answer exactly what is asked. The end of the sentence mentions "shorebirds and other wildlife." Choice F connects with that information better than the other options.

55. **C**. Again, we answer exactly what the question asks. In sentences 1 – 4 the passage gives facts about white water kayaks. In sentence 5 the author begins talking about sea kayaks. We should start a new paragraph at sentence 5 in order to "differentiate between the two types of kayaks."

56. **G**. ACT tries to trick you into thinking the subject of the sentence is the "kayaks," and therefore the sentence should read "kayaks are similar." This is incorrect because the subject of the sentence is the "equipment." Thus, "Equipment… is similar" is correct. Make sure you read the entire sentence while completing all the English Test questions. It's easy to make mistakes when you only look at the words around the underline. Furthermore, note that, as usual, the correct answer simply sounds right.

57. **B**. Choices A and D are grammatically incorrect. Choice A connects two full sentences with a comma (a period or semicolon would be needed instead). Choice D runs on without any necessary pauses. C is grammatically correct, but does not make sense. It would be like saying, 'Baseball players use a glove, so they wear long socks.' Choice B is the only acceptable answer.

58. **J**. Put the underlined phrase in each spot and read the resulting sentences. J creates the best, most readable sentence. Don't be afraid to take a little extra time on unusual questions like this one.

59. **B**. This sentence flows best without any pauses. If you chose A, recall that <u>if you are unsure about using a comma, it probably should be left out</u> (page 13). Furthermore, choices A and C are very similar, and they certainly cannot both be correct.

60. **G**. Choice G fits the entire paragraph best. While F and H have some merit, there certainly was not a "detailed description" or a "scientific explanation" anywhere in the paragraph. Be careful of strong words like those in this kind of question.

Passage V

61. **C**. Read the entire sentence. Inserting any commas (pauses) into this phrase would create awkward stops in the flow of the sentence.

62. **J**. While the other options may not sound perfect, J is grammatically incorrect. "Waking after centuries…" does not have a subject and is not a complete sentence. Take your time on 'NOT or LEAST acceptable questions,' rushing to answers leads to mistakes.

63. **C**. This demonstrates the concept of parallelism (see page 25). We want to keep the verbs in the same style. Therefore, "to feed and to breed" is correct.

64. **H**. Choice H avoids the wordiness of F and G and uses much clearer language than J.

65. **B**. First of all, *too* is correct in this situation. Consult a grammar website if you are unsure of the difference between *to* and *too*. Next, B is better than C because there would be no pause in speech after the word "poisonous." "…too poisonous to sustain life…" should not be interrupted; adding a comma would upset the flow of the sentence.

66. G. "called extremophiles" is an extra piece of information added into the sentence. Thus, we put a comma on each side of the phrase. Note that this could have also been written with no commas at all, as the sentence would also flow well with no pauses.

67. D. Choice D creates a run of two sentences combined without any punctuation; it is grammatically incorrect. Notice that B presents a good example of the use of dashes. It uses the dash as an interruption, a way to build tension between related thoughts. See page 21 for more on dashes.

68. J. Looking back to the last paragraph, we see that the author talks about these life forms in the present tense. Choice F would be correct if the extremophiles had gone extinct, but that is not the case.

69. D. Choices A, B, and C add information that has no relation to the focus of the passage. Keep it simple.

70. G. Choice G makes perfect sense if we read ahead a sentence (<u>when in doubt, read more</u> – see page 15). Furthermore, the explanations for F, H, and J are simply not true.

71. A. Choice A gives the most "specific" and "vivid" description of the terrain by using the word "scarred" instead of the more general terms in B, C, and D. As always, pay very close attention to the wording on this kind of question – a "specific and vivid" description is the only criteria for the correct answer.

72. J. Read the sentence with the underlined phrase in each spot. Answer J makes the sentence sound correct when read out loud.

73. A. Read the entire paragraph, and then read through each answer. Choice A is the only answer that does not mention the fact that psychrophiles are found in very cold conditions. Additionally, A is the only choice that does not mention that a psychrophile is a type of extremophile. Thus, A is the weakest option. Remember to always read ahead on questions like this one (see page 16).

74. G. This statement seems to fit well in the sentence, but as with all 'kept vs. deleted questions,' we still want to check out all the options. The explanations for F, H, and J are simply false. Choice G makes rational sense, especially if we read ahead to the last sentence of the paragraph. If you missed this one, read the passage a bit more carefully and determine why the explanations of F, H, and J are false.

75. D. This is a classic 'transition word question.' Choice D is the only option that makes sense when connecting the previous sentence to this one. Read those two sentences closely if you missed this one. See page 16 for more on transition word questions.

Note: Several of the above explanations say one answer "sounds the best" or "makes the sentence sound correct when read out loud." If you had trouble with these questions, the best (and easiest) way to improve is by reading more newspapers, magazines, and books. Even 10 minutes a day of reading will help.

Test 64E – Math Answers and Explanations

1. **D**. These straight lines indicate *absolute value*. In absolute values problems, you simply make a negative number inside of the lines into a positive. A positive number stays the same.

$$|4| - |-4| = 4 - 4 = 0$$

Common Mistake: Remember to do the math inside of the brackets prior to turning the negative to a positive. $|7 - 3| = |4|$, NOT $|7 + 3|$

2. **G**. This is a very common problem. We have one price that is always the same (the fixed price), and another price that goes up by the hour (the variable price).

$$\$30 + \$45X = \$210 \; (where \; X = the \; number \; of \; hours)$$

$$45X = 180$$

$$X = 4$$

Other Method: You could work backwards from the answers on this one, finding the cost of her work for each of the choices. However, this would be more time consuming. If you do work backwards, be sure to start with choice C. Since C is the middle answer choice, you will quickly figure out if you need more or less hours – this will eliminate two choices right away and save time.

3. **C**. We are given the mileage and the miles per gallon, now we have to find the total gallons used for each vehicle and compare them.

$$Vehicle \; A: \; 1008 \; miles / 14 \; miles \; per \; gallon = 72 \; gallons \; used$$

$$Vehicle \; B: \; 1008 \; miles / 36 \; miles \; per \; gallon = 28 \; gallons \; used$$

$$Difference \; between \; vehicles \; A \; and \; B: \quad 72 \; gallons - 28 \; gallons = 44 \; gallons$$

Couldn't get this one? Don't immediately rush to write an equation. Think about what you are computing and try to find a reason for your equation. Really try to determine why division is the logical way to solve this problem.

Chose answer B or E? Pay close attention to exactly what the question is asking!

4. **J**. This uses the basic algebra concept of 'combining like terms.' Review the concept if you missed this one. To solve this, let's first group the like terms:

$$t^2 - 82t^2 = -81t^2 \quad , \quad -59t + 60t = +t \quad , \quad +54 = +54$$

Now we put it all together: $\quad -81t^2 + t + 54$

5. C. We must know a few basic rules for this one. First we have to know that a square has 4 sides of the same length. Secondly, we must know that an equilateral triangle has 3 sides of the same length. Finally, we have to know that perimeter is the distance all the way around the outside of a shape.

So, we simply add up all the lengths on the outside of the shape to determine perimeter.

All of the sides of the square and equilateral triangle equal 6. Since 5 of these sides are on the outside of the figure, the perimeter = $6 \times 5 = 30$

Common mistake: E to B equals 6, so many students think the answer should be 36. E to B is not on the outside of the shape, though, so it is not included in perimeter.

6. J. This problem uses the math concept of *FOIL* to arrive at the answer. Review *FOIL* if you missed this one.

$$(4z + 3)(z - 2) = 4z^2 - 8z + 3z - 6$$

$$4z^2 - 5z - 6$$

7. C. This question tests your basic algebra skills and your knowledge of percentages. First of all, remember that 40% of a number just equals .40 times that number. Next we just have to follow the problem's language and make an equation from it.

40% of a number is 8 in equation form: $\quad .40(X) = 8$

Solving for X, we get: $\quad X = 8/.40 = 20$

Now we find 15% of that number: $\quad .15(20) = 3$

8. H. This one may look complicated, but remember that the Math Test starts easy and gets harder as it goes. All this problem really says is that if we add up the items in the list we get 447. Let's solve for X:

So, we add up the list and set it equal to 447: $\quad X - 2 + X - 1 + X + X + 1 + X + 2 + X + 3 = 447$

Combining like terms: $\quad 6X + 3 = 447$

Do the algebra to find X: $\quad X = 444/6 \quad X = 74$

9. D. The key to this question is, of course, to know the midpoint formula (see page 35). The midpoint formula appears on nearly every test. Also, we must realize that we've been given the midpoint and one end instead of the two ends. Therefore, we apply the formula a little bit differently than normal.

$$\frac{7+x}{2} = 5 \quad , \quad \frac{3+y}{2} = 4$$

Solving for X, we cross multiply to get: $\quad 7 + X = 10 \quad , \quad X = 3$

Solving for Y, we get: $\quad\quad\quad\quad\quad\quad 3 + Y = 8 \quad , \quad Y = 5$

Alternate Method: All Midpoints make sense logically. By that I mean that the X coordinate of the midpoint is literally in the middle of the two X coordinates of the endpoints. Same goes for the Y coordinates. To clarify, look to our previous example. Notice that 5 (the X coordinate of the midpoint) is two units away from both 7 and 3 (the X coordinates of the endpoints). That logic will work for Y as well.

10. **G**. The best way to attack this one is by plotting each of the answer choices to see which one fits. After plotting each point, it is evident that (9, -2) would make the fourth corner of a nice, symmetrical rectangle. Although ACT's drawings are not officially to scale, they are pretty darn close. Don't be afraid to choose an answer off of the picture.

Alternate Method: Although it would take a lot more time, you could solve this problem using either the distance or slope formula.

11. **E**. This problem looks scary with the matrices and all, but by reading the directions carefully, we find that it is not as bad as it looks. Basically these matrices are just little tables showing how many of each T-shirt is in each store and the cost of each brand of shirt. For example, there are 200 T-shirts of brand B in store X. Here is how the math would play out:

$$220 \; total \; of \; shirt \; A \; \times \$5 \; per \; shirt = \$1100 \; in \; shirt \; A \; inventory$$

$$250 \; total \; of \; shirt \; B \; \times \$10 \; per \; shirt = \$2500 \; in \; shirt \; B \; inventory$$

$$250 \; total \; of \; shirt \; C \; \times \$15 \; per \; shirt = \$3750 \; in \; shirt \; C \; inventory$$

Add them all up to get: $\;\; \$1100 + \$2500 + \$3750 = \$7350 \; total \; value \; of \; T-shirt \; inventory$

12. **J**. There usually are two or three problems similar to this one on each ACT Math Test, and the rules involved are not difficult to learn (see page 35). Here we have to know that a straight line adds to $180°$ and that a triangle adds to $180°$.

First, let's fill in the missing angle inside of the triangle. Although the question doesn't ask for this one, it is good to fill in any angles you can figure out, as they may be helpful in determining the values of other angles.

Since the triangle adds to $180°$: $\quad\quad\quad\quad\quad 180° - 57° - 72° = 51°$

Now, by using the law that a straight line is $180°$ we can figure out X, Y, and Z.

$$X = 180° - 57° = 123°$$

$$Y = 180° - 72° = 108°$$

$$Z = 180° - 51° = 129°$$

Since the question asked for the sum of X, Y, and Z: $\quad\quad 123° + 108° + 129° = 360°$

Note: This also could be solved by simply knowing that a polygon's exterior angles always add to 360°.

13. **A**. Percentages show up on the ACT often. Review them if you have trouble with these problems.

Here is the basic percentage formula as it relates to this question:

$$Percent\ Choosing\ Whitney = \frac{Number\ of\ Voters\ for\ Whitney}{Total\ Voters} \times 100\%$$

$$Percent\ Choosing\ Whitney = \frac{30}{200} = .15 = 15\%$$

Note: Any question looking for a basic percentage will be set up similarly to this one.

14. **H**. There are two ways to solve this problem; Check them both out, as the methods can be used on many different types of questions.

Ratio technique:

80 of the 200 people polled said they would vote for Lue; now we need to find how many out of 10,000 will vote for Lue. Whenever we can make a comparison like this one, ratios are an effective way to reach an answer.

We are told that the results follow the pattern of the poll, so we can set the ratios equal to each other:

$$\frac{80\ voters\ for\ Lue}{200\ total\ voters} = \frac{X\ voters\ for\ Lue}{10000\ total\ voters}$$

Now we cross-multiply and solve for X:

$$200X = 800000 \qquad X = \frac{80000}{200} \qquad X = 4000\ voters$$

Note: If you are unfamiliar with cross-multiplication, look it up and review the concept.

Percent Technique:

First we find the percentage of voters who are voting for Lue (same technique as in #13):

$$Percent\ voting\ for\ Lue = \frac{80\ voters\ for\ Lue}{200\ total\ voters} = .40 = 40\%$$

Now we know that 40% of voters are choosing Lue. So, to find the number of Lue votes out of 10,000, we just need to find 40% of 10,000:

$$Voters\ for\ Lue = .40 \times 10000 = 4000\ voters$$

15. **B**. This type of question has shown up on many different tests over the years. Make sure you really understand this one. Again, percentages or ratios can be used to solve.

Background information: In the circle graph, every candidate has his own slice. The size of the slice will depend on how many votes the candidate gets. The angles of all the slices will add to 360°, because all circles add to 360°.

Ratios:

The chart says Gomez got 40 of the 200 votes. Let's see how big a slice of the circle graph that equals:

$$40 \text{ voters for Gomez} / 200 \text{ total voters} = X° \text{ for Gomez} / 360° \text{ total in the graph}$$

Now solve for X: $\quad 14400 = 200X \quad\quad X = 14400/200 \quad\quad X = 72°$

Percents:

First we find the percentage of votes Gomez received:

$$40 \text{ voters for Gomez} / 200 \text{ total voters} = .20 = 20\%$$

This will be the same percentage of the circle that belongs to Gomez. Since a whole circle is 360°, we need to find 20% of 360:

$$.20 \times 360° = 72°$$

16. **G**. Again there are two effective methods to solve this problem. The second method is easier, but check out the first as well; it illustrates a helpful technique.

Technique 1 - Making up 'dummy numbers' (see page 40):

It usually is easier to work with actual numbers than a description in words. As long as we follow the directions for the problem, dummy numbers will work here.

Let's say each side of the square is equal to four. Now the diagram looks like this:

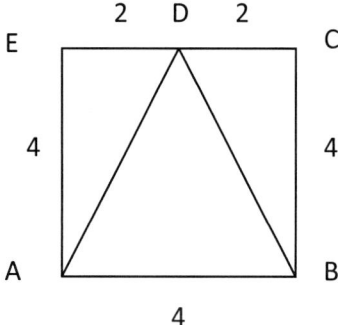

Note that line EC was split into 2 and 2 because D is the midpoint.

Now that we have actual numbers, we can literally compute the areas of the two triangles.

$$\text{Area of a Triangle} = \frac{1}{2}(base)(height)$$

Remember that the height of a triangle is the length from top to bottom, not the length of one of the diagonal lines. Thus, the height of ΔADB is 4 (the length from D straight down to the bottom line).

$$\text{Area } \Delta ADE = \frac{1}{2}(4)(2) = 4 \qquad \text{Area } \Delta ADB = \frac{1}{2}(4)(4) = 8$$

$$\text{Ratio of } \Delta ADE \text{ to } \Delta ADB = 4:8 = 1:2$$

Note: Any dummy number would have led to the same results.

Technique 2 – Work with the picture:

As mentioned earlier, you can trust pictures on the ACT Math Test to be fairly accurate. In fact, sometimes working with the picture is the best way to solve a problem. On this question, try drawing a line straight down from point D to the bottom of the figure. You will find that ΔADB looks to be made up of two pieces that are identical to ΔADE. Therefore, G is the best answer.

17. **E**. Here we have to know a bit about lines:

First of all, in the form *Y=mX+B*, m is the slope. So the slope of the given line is $2/3$.

Next, parallel lines have the same slope, so the slope of a parallel line is also $2/3$.

18. **H**. This question requires solid basic algebra skills. It is best solved by creating an equation. You are certain to see similar questions on your upcoming ACT.

The ratio of the lengths is 2:3. Unfortunately, the entire board is not 2 + 3 = 5 feet long. We will need some multiple of the 2:3 ratio in order to make up a 30 foot board.

So our equation is: $\qquad 2X + 3X = 30$

Solving for X: $\qquad 5X = 30 \qquad X = 6$

We found X, but the smaller piece was actually 2X in the equation. Make sure you are answering the question they ask! The answer is: $2 \times 6 = 12 \text{ feet}$.

Alternate Method – Ratios:

$$\frac{2 \text{ feet (small piece)}}{5 \text{ feet (whole board)}} = \frac{X \text{ feet (small piece)}}{30 \text{ feet (whole board)}}$$

$$5X = 60 \qquad X = 12 \text{ feet}$$

Note: You could also try working backwards from the answers on this question.

19. **C**. An integer is any number that has no fraction or decimal attached to it. An integer can be negative, positive, or zero. Knowing that, this one is easily solved with a calculator.

Type in $\sqrt{58}$. Your calculator will display 7.615... The smallest integer greater than 7.6 is the next whole number up, 8.

20. **G**. This problem is a bit complicated, but it really just involves working with the area of a rectangle formula. Note that when the phrases *square feet, square inches, square meters,* etc. are used, it is probably an area problem.

A gallon covers between 300 and 350 square feet, so let's figure out how much area Sergio has to paint.

Each wall equals: $\qquad 10 \; feet \; \times 15 \; feet = 150 \; square \; feet$

For all four walls: $\qquad 150 \; square \; feet \; \times 4 \; walls = 600 \; square \; feet$

But we can subtract the area of the window and door because those areas do not need paint:
window: $3 \; feet \times 5 \; feet = 15 \; square \; feet \qquad$ door: $3.5 \; feet \; \times 7 \; feet = 24.5 \; square \; feet$

$$600 - 15 - 24.5 = 560.5 \; square \; feet \; that \; need \; paint$$

Since the gallons cover 300 to 350 square feet, Sergio needs at least two gallons to paint it all.

21. **A**. This question involves solving a quadratic function or to 'unFOIL.' Review quadratics if you forget the technique. Some calculator programs can solve these automatically, although it is best to understand the math.

First, we get everything to one side so the equation is in the form $\quad aX^2 + bX + c = 0$

$$X^2 + 2X - 8 = 0$$

Now we must find a pair of numbers that multiply to -8 (the number to the right), and add to 2 (the middle number). This method always works as long as there is no number in front of X^2.

Numbers that multiply to -8: $\qquad$ 8 and -1 $\qquad$ -8 and 1 $\qquad$ -4 and 2 $\qquad$ 4 and -2

Since 4 and -2 are the only pair that adds to 2, we will use them. The equation is rewritten:

$$(X + 4)(X - 2) = 0$$

The numbers that solve this correctly are -4 and 2.

Common mistake: If you chose C, you were on the right track but forgot the last step.

Alternate Method: Working backwards (substituting the answers for X and seeing which equal 8) would be effective on this problem, but it will not work every time. It is best to understand the math.

22. **K**. This question requires good knowledge of math involving fractions and variables.

We simplify fractions by dividing numbers or variables from both the top and bottom of the fraction.

For this fraction, we can divide a 3 from both the top and bottom:

$$\frac{3a^4 \div 3}{3a^6 \div 3} = \frac{a^4}{a^6}$$

We can also divide out a^4:

$$\frac{a^4 \div a^4}{a^6 \div a^4} = \frac{1}{a^2}$$

We cannot divide anything else out, so the answer is K.

23. **E**. Here we simply have to read the question carefully, and then use basic knowledge about graphs.

The directions say that at point M, X and Y both are not zero and have opposite signs.

X coordinates are only positive in quadrants I and IV. Y coordinates are only positive in I and II.

Quadrants II and IV have opposite signs for X and Y.

24. **K**. The $1,400 cost is going to happen every day whether 5 or 1,000,000 basketballs are made. The $1,400 does not depend on b (the number of basketballs made in a day). The $5.25 is the price per basketball; each time a new basketball is made, another $5.25 is spent. So, that will depend on b. More b (basketballs), means more times you have to spend $5.25. The final cost equals the daily $1,400 plus $5.25 for each basketball.

Note: If you missed this question, think through the answers logically, not just mathematically. Maybe try an example – say there were 10 basketballs made. Then determine which answer makes sense.

25. **B**. Similar triangles are fairly common on this test. A brief explanation of them is on page 32.

In similar triangles, perimeters and corresponding sides can be compared with a ratio. Here side AC corresponds to side KM. The perimeter of ΔKLM is 35. We can set up this ratio:

$$\text{Side AC}/\text{Perimeter } \Delta ABC = \text{Side KM}/\text{Perimeter } \Delta KLM \quad \rightarrow \quad 3/X = 7.5/35$$

Cross multiply and solve for X:

$$7.5X = 105 \qquad X = 105/7.5 \qquad X = 14$$

26. **G**. There are a few ways to solve this problem. The easiest way is to apply a mathematical rule.

The tops (numerators) of the fractions are already the same. To make these completely equal, we need to get the bottoms (denominators) to be identical as well. Thus, we need $a\sqrt{7}$ to equal 7.

The rule necessary to solve this is best illustrated through examples:

$$\sqrt{5} \times \sqrt{5} = 5 \qquad \sqrt{21} \times \sqrt{21} = 21 \qquad \sqrt{6} \times \sqrt{6} = 6$$

So, if $a = \sqrt{7}$, we get:

$$\frac{3\sqrt{7}}{\sqrt{7} \times \sqrt{7}} = \frac{3\sqrt{7}}{7} \qquad \rightarrow \qquad \frac{3\sqrt{7}}{7} = \frac{3\sqrt{7}}{7}$$

Alternate method: If you were unfamiliar with the rule here, good use of your calculator could still lead to the correct answer. You could cross multiply and solve for a, or you could work backwards from your answers to find the choice that makes the two fractions identical.

27. **C.** This is a common question type that requires solid algebra skills.

We have two balloons we will call F (the falling balloon) and R (the rising balloon).

The equation for Balloon F's height is: $\qquad height = 70\ meters - 6(X\ seconds)$

Seems logical, right? It is currently at 70 meters, but goes down 6 meters with each second that passes.

The equation for Balloon R's height is: $\qquad height = 10\ meters + 15(X\ seconds)$

We need to find when they have the same height, so we set the equations equal to each other:

$$70 - 6X = 10 + 15X$$

Solving for X: $\qquad 60 = 21X \qquad\qquad X = {}^{60}\!/_{21} \qquad\qquad X = 2.857$

Alternate method: If you forgot to set the equations equal to each other, you could still solve by working backwards from the answers. You could find the respective heights at each time, and then see which match up.

Note: Always be smart when working backwards, choices D and E (and possibly A) could be removed from consideration right away. Those answers just are not logical.

28. **J.** Most tests contain one of these combination questions. They are very easy (see page 36).

The group has 4 options for roads, 2 options for bike paths, and 6 options for trails.

Their total amount of routes: $\qquad 4 \times 2 \times 6 = 48\ different\ routes$

29. **E.** This question demonstrates the importance of knowing the formulas. If you know the volume of a cube formula, you get it right; if you don't know the formula, you probably take a guess.

Cube B's edges are double Cube A's edges, so they are equal to 4.

$$Volume\ of\ a\ cube = Side^{\,3}$$

Cube B's sides are 4, so: $\qquad Volume\ of\ Cube\ B = 4^3 = 64\ cubic\ inches$

30. **G**. This type of question also appears on the ACT somewhat often. ACT always gives you the formula and the definition of each variable, but it still helps to practice a couple of these.

$$A = P(1 + r)^n$$

We are given P (the $10,000 deposited), r (4%), and n (5 years). We are looking for A (current value of the account).

$$A = 10000(1 + .04)^5$$

Following the order of operations, we add what is in the parentheses, and then take that number to the exponent.

$$A = \quad 10000(1.04)^5 \quad = \quad 10000(1.2167)$$

Finally we multiply to get the answer: $10000(1.2167) = \$12,167$

Common mistake: Remember 4% = .04 not .40   .40 is 40%

31. **D**. On this question, we simply have to plug numbers into the given formula. If you are given a formula on the ACT Math Test, use it. They are not trying to trick you.

On the figure, the height is 20 and the radius is 10 (half the given diameter of 20). Let's plug those in:

$$Surface\ Area = 2\pi(10^2) + 2\pi(10)(20) \quad = \quad 200\pi + 400\pi \quad = \quad 600\pi\ square\ centimeters$$

Note: If you had multiplied the numbers on the calculator instead of keeping the pi separate, you would have gotten: $628.31 + 1256.64 = 1884.95$. Testing each answer, you will find that 600π also equals 1884.95.

32. **H**. This kind of problem appears on many tests; review *function notation* if you forget the concept. These problems involve basic substitution and are not as difficult as they appear. Once you get the basics down, this concept is easily perfected with a little bit of practice.

The key is to work from the inside out, substituting what is inside the parenthesis for the X('s) in the function outside the parenthesis. In this example, *g(x)* is inside the parenthesis, and *f* is outside.

So here we substitute *g(x)* in for the X in *f(x)*:

$$f\big(g(X)\big) = 4(X^2 - 2) + 1$$

$$f\big(g(X)\big) = \ 4X^2 - 8 + 1 \quad = \quad 4X^2 - 7$$

Common Mistake: Many students choose answer J. When you substitute *g(x)* in for the X, the 4 must be distributed across the whole function, not just to the X^2 term.

33. **B**. The key to any average problem is to remember the simple definition of an average.

$$Average = \frac{Total\ Number\ of\ Points}{Number\ of\ Trials}$$

For this question, let's modify the wording slightly to say:

$$Average = \frac{Total\ Number\ of\ Goals}{Number\ of\ Games}$$

The directions say there are 43 games played, so all we need to do is add up the total amount of goals.

We had, for example, 2 goals scored in 5 games, so there were $2 \times 5 = 10\ goals$ in those games. We just need to apply that same logic to all of the data in the chart.

$$Total\ goals:\ 0(4) + 1(10) + 2(5) + 3(9) + 4(7) + 5(5) + 6(1) + 7(2) = 120\ goals$$

Now back to the formula:

$$Average = \frac{120\ total\ goals}{43\ games} = 2.8\ goals\ per\ game$$

Note: Even if you could not figure out this question mathematically, you should be able to eliminate every answer choice except B and C. Looking at the data, it is clear that choice A is too low of an average and D and E are too high.

34. **H.** Angles are supplementary if they add up to 180º. Review angle terminology if you need to refresh your knowledge.

First, we know angles 1 and 2 are supplementary with X because all straight lines add to 180º.

Next, by the rules of alternate interior and alternate exterior (or by the rule of corresponding angles), angles 1 and 2 are equal to angles 9 and 10. So if 1 and 2 are supplementary, 9 and 10 must be as well.

None of angles 4 – 7 or angles 12 – 15 are supplementary. Line D is at a completely different angle than line C. Although they both pass through parallel lines, lines C and D really don't have anything else in common. Also, remember to trust the picture. Those angles just do not look to be supplementary.

Note: If you forget rules like alternate interior, just try to find angles that look the same. It is OK to trust the pictures on this test.

35. **E.** If you missed this one, review exponent rules in an Algebra book or online.

$3^3 = 27$ $(X^3)^3 = X^{3 \times 3} = X^9$ Putting it all together: $27X^9$

36. **F.** Inequalities are not as difficult as they may seem. The solving process is basically the same as in a normal algebra problem with an equal sign. The only difference is that when **multiplying or dividing by a negative number, the < or > sign flips the opposite way.**

$$4X - 8 > 8X + 16$$

Subtract 4X and 16 from each side. Then divide by 4 to get X by itself.

$$-24 > 4X \qquad -6 > X \qquad \text{Which is the exact same as: } X < -6$$

If you had instead subtracted 8X and then added 16 to each side, you would be left with:

$$-4X > 24$$

Now, when you divide by -4, you must also flip the sign.

$$X < \frac{24}{-4} \qquad X < -6$$

37. **C**. These questions about rotations, although a bit strange, show up on many ACTs. They involve logic and sometimes some math skills. The first step in solving these is to visualize the rotation.

On this question, the point is rotated 90° clockwise – that is a quarter of the way around the 360° circle. By basic estimation, it seems the point would end up somewhere near the bottom right arc of the circle. Now let's look to the answers.

Choice A is the center. It is not a point on the circle so it is out of consideration. Choice B is inside of the circle, so it is out. Choices C and D both are near the bottom right arc and can be considered. Choice E is only a short rotation from P, not 90°, so it is out.

Now draw a line from point P to the center and lines from the center to choices C and D. The line to (5,-1) seems to complete a perfect 90° angle. The one to (6,0) caves in a bit and looks to be less than 90°. Furthermore, notice that the line to (5,-1) (along with the line from the center to P) divides the circle into a perfect quarter. The line to (6,0) seems to be smaller than one fourth of the entire circle. Thus, (5,-1) is where point P would be after a 90° rotation.

Note: There are mathematical methods to solving rotations, but considering that there is a maximum of one rotation problem per test, they are not necessary to learn (visualizing it works anyway!).

38. **K**. This question combines two very important concepts, the Pythagorean Theorem and SOHCAHTOA.

Based on SOHCAHTOA: $\qquad \sin M = {Opposite}/{Hypotenuse}$

The hypotenuse is clearly 12, but no value is given for the side opposite angle M. However, when one side length is missing in a right triangle, we can use the Pythagorean Theorem to solve for it.

In the Pythagorean formula, 'a' will be side ML, 'b' will serve as missing side KL, and 'c' by rule will be the hypotenuse, which is side MK. ('a' and 'b' are interchangeable, but 'c' must be the hypotenuse)

$$a^2 + b^2 = c^2 \qquad\qquad 10^2 + b^2 = 12^2$$

$$100 + b^2 = 144 \qquad b^2 = 44 \qquad b = \sqrt{44}$$

Now we can find the sin of M:

$$\sin M = {Opposite}/{Hypotenuse} = {\sqrt{44}}/{12}$$

39. **B**. This question is tough, but by thinking outside the box a bit, we can prove the answer fairly easily.

First of all, choice B just seems to look right. We have a straight line (180°) that appears to be divided into 3 equally symmetrical parts of 60°. However, we probably still want to prove this one, and we can do so by working backwards and trying out other answers.

Let's try choice A, 90°. Paying close attention to the directions, we see that BD bisects angle ABE, and that BE bisects angle CBD. "Bisect" means that the line divides the angle in half, and we are left with two identical angles on either side of the bisector.

So if angle DBE is 90°, the angles on the other sides of the bisectors would also have to be 90°.

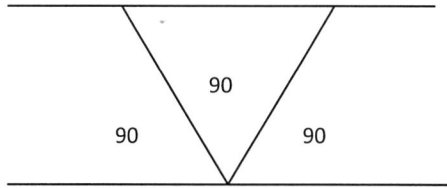

This picture cannot be correct. The straight line must add to 180° and this adds to 270°.

By now you may realize that 60° will be the only acceptable answer. If not, try one or two more choices just as we did with choice A. You will quickly realize that 60° is the only angle measure that can work.

Alternate Method: The most direct way to solve this problem would be with the 'transitive' or 'substitution' properties of geometry. Since angle ABD = angle DBE and angle DBE = angle EBC (both due to the definition of a bisector), then angle ABD = angle EBC. All three angles are equal and together add to 180°. They must all be 60°.

40. **H**. Here ACT asks for the number of molecules per cubic centimeter. This means we have to divide the number of molecules by the amount of cubic centimeters. Whenever you want ((A)) per ((B)), you always divide ((A)) by ((B)). The most common example of this is when determining miles per hour.

So the equation looks like: $\dfrac{8 \times 10^{12} \text{ molecules}}{4 \times 10^4 \text{ cubic centimeters}}$

This can easily be done in your graphing calculator, just be careful to use parenthesis around each number. It should look like this in your calculator: (8 * 10^12) / (4 * 10^4)

This will return the answer 200000000. A 2 with eight 0's can be rewritten as 2×10^8. If you forgot how to work with scientific notation, look it up; it is easy to relearn.

Note: When in doubt, always put parenthesis around functions, fractions, etc. on your calculator.

41. **B**. This law of cosines problem is fairly complicated, although the diagram does clear things up a bit. Whenever the law of cosines appears on this test, the formula will be given to you. Still, knowing about the law beforehand makes the problem much easier.

On this problem, every answer choice is the same except for the angle at the end. The correct choice is B because the angle across from the triangle side we need (the distance between the boats) equals $300° - 170° = 130°$.

Looking deeper at the formula: $a = 30$, $b = 20$, $c = $ distance between boats, angle $C = 130°$

All law of cosine problems set up similarly to this one. You are given side, angle, side – and you have to solve for the third side. The given sides are always a and b, and the missing side is always c. If you have worked with the law of cosines before, it is worth relearning. If you have not, it is probably best to just guess on problems like this one. They are not very common anyway.

42. **J**. This problem can either be solved with common denominators or with good use of your calculator.

<u>Common denominators</u>: Getting a common denominator is a good idea whenever you are comparing fractions. Just make sure you multiply the top and bottom of the fraction by the same number.

$$\frac{1 \times 3}{5 \times 3} = \frac{3}{15} \qquad \frac{1 \times 5}{3 \times 5} = \frac{5}{15}$$

Looking to our answers, it is pretty clear that $\frac{4}{15}$ would be right in the middle of these two.

To prove it we can use the midpoint formula, which always works to find the middle number:

$$\frac{(\frac{5}{15} + \frac{3}{15})}{2} = \frac{(\frac{8}{15})}{2} = \frac{4}{15}$$

<u>Calculator Method</u>: Type the fractions into your calculator. You get the following results:

$$\frac{1}{5} = .20 \qquad \frac{1}{3} = .3333\ldots$$

Now try the answer choices. To save time, skip any that you already know are wrong. You get:

$$\frac{1}{2} = .5 \qquad \frac{1}{4} = .25 \qquad \frac{2}{15} = .133\ldots \qquad \frac{4}{15} = .267\ldots \qquad \frac{8}{15} = .533\ldots$$

Only .25 and .267 are between .20 and .333. With some basic arithmetic we can determine that .267, not .25, is halfway between the numbers.

43. **B**. The key to this question is realizing that, just as the picture appears, isosceles trapezoids have symmetrical diagonals. From there, we just have to know a few rules about angle measures. For this explanation we will call the center point where the diagonals cross "P."

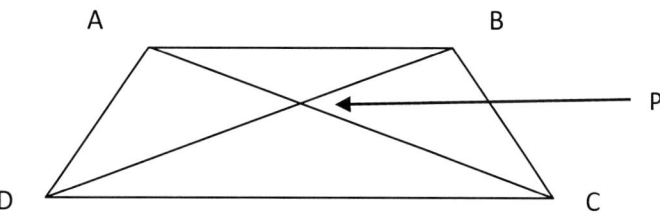

First our givens (fill these in as you go): **Angle BDC = 25°** , **Angle BCA = 35°**

Next, **Line DP = Line CP** - In an isosceles trapezoid, diagonals are divided into segments that are congruent to the segments across from them (so Line BP = Line AP as well). In general, things tend to be very symmetrical in isosceles trapezoids (search online to find a full listing of isosceles trapezoid laws).

So, **Angle PDC = Angle PCD = 25°** - Triangle PDC has two sides that are the same; whenever two triangle sides are the same, the two angles across from them are the same as well.

Angle DPC = 130° - The angles in triangle PDC add to 180°.

Angle BPC = 50° - All straight lines add to 180°.

Finally, **Angle DBC = 95°** - The angles in triangle BPC add to 180°.

44. **G**. This problem requires sound knowledge of square roots and a bit of logic.

$$Area\ of\ a\ square = side^2$$

First we solve for the length of a side of each square:

Larger square: $S^2 = 50$ $\quad\quad S = \sqrt{50} \quad\quad S = 5\sqrt{2}$

Smaller square: $S^2 = 18$ $\quad\quad S = \sqrt{18} \quad\quad S = 3\sqrt{2}$

X is the difference between the smaller and larger sides so: $\quad\quad X = 5\sqrt{2} - 3\sqrt{2} = 2\sqrt{2}$

Note: Review square roots if any of this math was difficult for you.

Alternate method: If you are shaky with the math involving square roots, you can use your calculator to get the answer in a decimal. Then you can go through the answers to see what matches up.

45. E. Irrational numbers are numbers with decimals that go on forever without any sort of pattern. Any number that, when simplified, still has a square root involved is irrational. Pi is also irrational. Every other number you see on the ACT Math Test is rational.

On this problem, choices A, B, and C are simplified and still involve a square root, so they are irrational.

Choice D can be simplified: $\sqrt{\frac{5}{25}} = \frac{\sqrt{5}}{\sqrt{25}} = \frac{\sqrt{5}}{5}$ but in the end it still has a square root and is irrational.

Choice E can be simplified: $\sqrt{\frac{64}{49}} = \frac{\sqrt{64}}{\sqrt{49}} = \frac{8}{7}$ in the end there is no square root; it is rational.

46. K. On this question, it is helpful to make up your own 'dummy numbers' for a and b. You can use any numbers, as long as you follow the direction that $a < b$. Trying to solve this just using variables would be much more difficult.

So, let's say $a = 3$, $b = 5$. Then: $|a - b| = |3 - 5| = 2$

Now we test the answers to find which choice also equals 2.

Choice K would be: $-(3 - 5) = 2$ It is the only choice that also equals 2, so it must be correct.

Note: Occasionally more than one answer choice will work out. If this happens, change the dummy numbers and try again.

47. A. As with most averaging problems, the easiest way to complete this one is with the simple equation for averages.

$$Average = \frac{Total\ Points}{Number\ of\ Trials}$$

Let's start by looking at where Tom is now, after five tests:

$$78.0 = \frac{X\ points}{5\ trials}$$

We can solve for his point total with basic algebra: $78.0 \times 5 = 390\ points$

Now let's look at where Tom would be if he can get his average up to an 80:

$$80.0 = \frac{x\ points}{6\ trials}$$

Again we solve for the missing number, the point total: $80 \times 6 = 480\ points$

So, through five tests Tom has 390 points. To get to the 80 average by the sixth test, he needs 480 points. He needs $480 - 390 = 90\ points$ on the sixth test.

48. **F.** This looks scary, but if you can decipher the directions, the problem proves to be easier than it seems. Remember that this test does not go past basic trigonometry; the math involved in these questions often is not as bad as it looks.

The question asks for the point on this graph that has the greatest *modulus*. Fortunately, the question also tells us that the *modulus* is equal to $\sqrt{a^2 + b^2}$. If we look past all the complicated talk of complex numbers, we see a fairly straightforward statement saying that the point (a,b) can be read just like a normal (X,Y) point. Thus, point z_1, which has the highest Y axis value and a large negative value on the X axis (this will get squared and turn positive), would have the highest value for $\sqrt{a^2 + b^2}$.

Note: This is not a common problem to see on the ACT, but it demonstrates a valuable concept. On more difficult problems, find a way to make it work. Find a formula to apply, find a way to eliminate some answers or, as on this question, find a way to simplify the problem. With a little creative thinking your chances of choosing the correct answer rise greatly.

49. **C.** The fastest way to complete this problem is through strong knowledge of exponent algebra. The simplest way to complete this is through classic guess and check. Either way will work well.

Mathematical solution:

$$8^{2x+1} = 4^{1-x}$$

Since $2^3 = 8$ and $2^2 = 4$, we can rewrite the equation like this:

$$2^{3(2x+1)} = 2^{2(1-x)}$$

Both of the base numbers are now 2, so we can set the exponents equal to each other and solve for x:

$3(2x + 1) = 2(1 - x)$ $6x + 3 = 2 - 2x$ $8x = -1$ $x = \frac{-1}{8}$

Guess and check solution:

Generally it is best to start at answer C and, if it is incorrect, determine whether you need to move to a higher or lower number. Unfortunately, this technique would not be all that effective on a question like this one. Still, we can eliminate some answers through basic exponent knowledge.

The first two choices to eliminate probably are D and E. Using some exponent knowledge, we know this:

$$8^{2(0)+1} \neq 4^{1-0} \quad and \quad 8^{\frac{2}{7}+1} \neq 4^{1-\frac{1}{7}}$$

After testing the other options with a calculator, we find:

$$8^{2\left(\frac{-1}{8}\right)+1} = 4.757 \quad and \quad 4^{1+\frac{1}{8}} = 4.757 \quad so\ C\ must\ be\ correct$$

Note: Entering these complicated expressions in your calculator can be rough. Sometimes it is best to break the problem into pieces, find smaller parts on your calculator, and then put it all together. Storing numbers with the 'STO' button (bottom left corner) on your TI graphing calculator can help with this.

50. **F**. Occasionally you will see one trigonometry graph question near the end of the Math Test. Often, as in this problem, the directions tell you how to solve the problem algebraically. Still, the language used can be difficult to understand, so a basic understanding of sin and cos graphs is beneficial.

On this problem, it is essential to know what f(x) means in relation to a graph:

f(x) = the value of Y at a given value of X. For example, f(0) = where Y is on the graph when X=0. On this problem, f(0) = 2, because when X=0, Y=2. By the same logic, it appears that f(6) = −2 and f(−6)= −2. Look over the examples closely if you do not understand – the concept is easier than it may seem.

Now that we have an understanding of f(x), we can prove F to be the correct answer choice:

Let's test a few values: $f(3) = 0, f(-3) = 0$ $\quad\quad f(6) = -2, f(-6) = -2$

By now you may begin to see the pattern in the graph: $f(x)\ equals\ f(-x)\ throughout\ the\ curve.$

51. **D**. This question requires sound logic more than any math skills. Let's try to figure it out:

First, we'll figure out how many numbers from 100 – 199 have a 0 as a digit:

100 – 109 (10 numbers), 110, 120, 130, 140, 150, 160, 170, 180, and 190. A total of 19 numbers between 100 and 199 have a zero as a digit.

With a little more logic, we can determine that the list will look the same for the 200s – 900s (except for the first digit of course). Thus, $19\ numbers \times 9\ sets = 171\ numbers\ with\ 0\ as\ a\ digit$. Since there are 900 total numbers between 100 and 999, the answer is D.

52. **F**. This is a difficult question, although some choices can be quickly eliminated. Line *r* is downward sloping, so H and J, positive slopes, can be eliminated right away. Choice G can also be disregarded. If you plot a line with a slope of $-1/2$ you will find that it is much flatter than line *r*. This leaves us with only F and K as potential correct answers. First of all, based on the equation in the directions, line q's slope is 2. Given that fact, analyzing the picture probably gives enough evidence to choose F. It appears that line r has the same slope as line q; it's just moving in the opposite direction. If you tilted the line a little bit (changed the slope), the two angles would no longer be congruent. Choice F makes sense. Using logic is important when you get to difficult questions like this one.

Note: The mathematical reason for the answer is because lines with the same slope, whether it is negative or positive, cross a horizontal line at the same angle.

53. **D**. This question takes SOHCAHTOA to a more difficult level. While questions like this are not as common as basic SOHCAHTOA problems like #38, they do show up occasionally.

The first part of the problem is to solve $tan^{-1}(\frac{a}{b})$:

This is an *inverse tangent*. It is basically asking, 'for which angle does $tan = \frac{a}{b}$?'

To solve, we use SOHCAHTOA backwards. Since $tan = opp./adj.$, the far right angle is the one that would have $tan = \frac{a}{b}$.

Now we have to find the cosine of that angle. Since $cos = adj./hyp.$, and we are working from the far right angle, $cos = b/\sqrt{a^2 + b^2}$.

Note: Even if you missed the first part of the question, C and D would be the best answer choices to guess. Why? We were looking for cos, which means hypotenuse has to be in the denominator.

54. **J**. The coverage area is a circle with radius = 52.

$Area\ of\ a\ circle = \pi r^2$ $\qquad$ $Area = \pi \times 52^2$ $\qquad$ $Area = 8495\ square\ miles$

55. **E**. The equation of a circle shows up once on most tests. It is an easy concept, so take the time to learn it (see page 33).

This circle is centered at the origin (0,0) in the plane. So the left side of the equation must be:

$(x - 0)^2 + (y - 0)^2$ $\qquad$ or just $\qquad$ $x^2 + y^2$

The radius is 52. So, by definition, the right side of the equation must be: 52^2 $\quad$ *(radius squared)*

56. **G**. This question is simplified by carefully drawing a diagram.

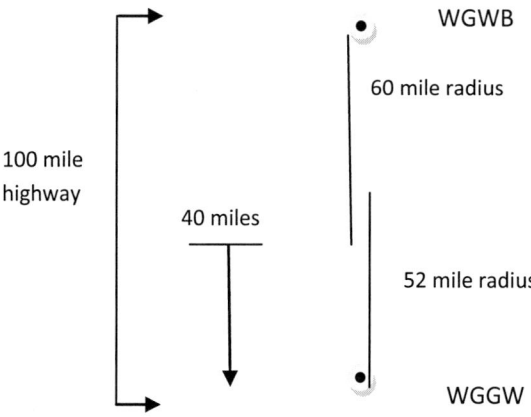

Now we just have to logic it out from the picture. If we were driving down the highway from WGGW to WGWB, we'd hit WGWB's signal after 40 miles. At this point we'd still have 12 miles left with WGGW's signal.

57. E. Here they are simply asking, for what values of X is $(x-1)^4 < (x-1)$. You can determine this through math knowledge or by simply looking at the graph.

<u>Math knowledge</u>: The only time a positive number gets smaller as it is taken to a positive integer exponent is if the number is between 0 and 1. Choice E gives us this situation.

<u>Graph</u>: The graph plainly shows that $(x-1)^4$ produces a lower result than $(x-1)$ in the area between $x=1$ and $x=2$.

58. F. It is essential to use dummy numbers to solve this question (see page 40).

Let's say $x=35$, so $t=3$ and $u=5$

Thus, following the directions closely: $y = 53$

So what is equivalent to $x-y$ or $35 - 53 = -18$

$$F) = 9(3-5) = -18 \qquad G) = 9(5-3) = 18$$

$$H) = 9(3) - 5 = 22 \qquad J) = 9(5) - 3 = 42 \qquad K) = 0$$

Answer F is the only one that matches up; it is the only choice that could be equivalent to $x-y$

59. A. $\text{Area of a triangle} = \frac{1}{2}(base) \times (height)$

Finding the base and height is an easy task as we are moving in straight lines on the graph. The distance formula is not necessary. It is only needed when finding the length of diagonal lines.

Base = 4; the base stretches straight across 4 units from (1,3) to (5,3)

Height = 2; the bottom of the triangle is on the line Y=3. The top is at the line Y=5. A straight line from top to bottom is 2 units (straight up from Y=3 to Y=5)

$$\text{Area} = \frac{1}{2}(4)(2) = 4$$

60. F. We can begin this problem by filling in the equation's variables with the information given.

$$\text{Sum} = \frac{a}{1-r} \qquad \text{Sum} = 200 \qquad r = .15$$

$$200 = \frac{a}{1 - .15} \qquad a = 200 \times .85 = 170$$

So we solved for *a*, the missing variable. But *a* is defined as the first term in the sequence. The question asked for the second term.

To get the next term in the sequence we must multiply by the common ratio.

$$170 \times .15 = 25.5 \; (the\; second\; term)$$

If you did not understand this, you may want to review geometric sequences and common ratios; they are not too difficult to understand and they do show up occasionally on the ACT.

Final note: This is an actual ACT Math Test, but, frankly, it is slightly easier than your average Math Test. Keep challenging yourself, taking practice tests, and reviewing math concepts. The best way to improve your score is by completing practice problems and learning from any mistakes you make.

Test 64E – Reading Answers and Explanations – Reading Method.

Passage I – Prose Fiction

1. **B**. As usual, the first question asks about the big picture of the passage. Choice B gives the most accurate depiction of the story as a whole. This passage is mostly about the woman who cannot dream, and we learn about her through her conversations with the narrator. Each of the other choices contains some inaccuracy. Choice A is wrong because the one woman does not have any dreams. C is wrong because it portrays the narrator as some third person, which is not true — the narrator is the woman who dreams. D is wrong because we do not get a detailed description of several of the narrator's dreams; she only describes one dream in detail. As you can see, if even a small part of an answer choice is incorrect the choice can be eliminated from consideration.

2. **F**. First of all, look up any of these words if you are unsure of their meanings. While this is not a vocabulary test, ACT expects you to know 12th grade level words such as these. Now, once the words are defined, we see that choice F fits the passage best. The woman who cannot dream is certainly frustrated to the point of despair. Meanwhile, the narrator constantly tries to make the woman feel better, supporting and reassuring her throughout the passage. Choices G and J do not work mainly because of the characterization of the narrator. The narrator tries to be very nice and helpful; she is not "angry" or "uninterested." Choice H does not quite fit either, as "resigned" and "relaxed" are not as accurate as F's descriptions.

3. **B**. Based on the overall tone of the passage, choice B is best. The woman feels she is missing out on an almost spiritual learning experience by not dreaming. This fits "self-awareness" much better than the other options. If you were unsure of the answer, you could quickly look back to the text. Since this question asks about general introductory information, looking at the beginning of the passage would be a good starting point. Sure enough, lines 2 – 4 confirm B as the answer.

4. **J**. While you may not have completely picked up on the door metaphor, J just makes a lot of sense given the big picture of the essay. Remember that even questions about small facts often relate to the main ideas of the passage. This answer could be confirmed by reading lines 4 – 7 or 37 – 42, but if you are pretty confident in an answer you don't have to prove it in the text. Too much rereading will leave you short on time.

5. **C**. Glance at your answers, and then go back to the text. Don't be afraid to start reading a bit before line 10. It is helpful to read around the line numbers they mention — you get some context for the information in those lines. On this question reading extra is especially important, because the question says "in relation to the first paragraph's earlier description..." Now, based on the first paragraph, lines 10 – 13 clearly show the hopelessness the woman feels at being unable to break through the door to the world of dreams.

Note: Context is the information surrounding a word or phrase that can help you figure out what that word or phrase means.

6. **G**. You may remember that the amniotic dream was the favorite of the woman who cannot dream. If not, no problem, this question is fairly easy to look up in the text. If you look to the end of the passage where the amniotic dream is mentioned, line 71 confirms choice G. None of the other choices are supported by the text.

7. **D**. The woman mentions a couple of times that she feels different because she cannot dream. The paragraph at lines 31 – 34 is the most direct example. You could also get this answer by the process of elimination. Choice A and C do not make sense because the woman is absolutely desperate to dream. She never worries about dreaming too much or having nightmares. Choice B is not supported by anything in the text; the narrator is helpful and caring.

8. **J**. This is a question we will probably have to look up in the text. We begin looking near the end of the passage, as that is where the narrator tells the woman about her dreams. We find this answer in the first sentence of the paragraph beginning at line 53 (first sentences often contain key information). We see that the woman dreams the dream in "privacy," "with the lights out," "hiding." These words directly connect with choice J. Also note that J fits the characterization of the woman best; she is not "confident," "playful," or "powerful" anywhere in this essay, but she certainly is "self-conscious."

9. **C**. These definition questions show up a few times per test. The key is simply to read as much as you need to get context for the word. If we read lines 54 – 59, we see that the woman is irritated by her inability to dream, and this makes her envious and puts her in a bad mood.

10. **H**. This question regards a small fact you may remember or may have to look up. In lines 61 – 64, the narrator states that telling dreams is very difficult, and perhaps only Franz Kafka has done it effectively. If you did not remember reading that, a simple search for the name Franz Kafka (names are usually easy to find!) leads you to the correct information. Note that choices F and G contain words that match up to words found near Kafka's name in the text. This is a common trick: although the same words are used, these answers say something entirely different from the text. See page 76 for more on this.

Passage II – Social Science

11. **A**. This question is covered extensively in the final two paragraphs. While the language in those paragraphs is technical and sometimes difficult to understand, remember that the primary goal of the initial read is to understand the main ideas of the essay, not necessarily to grasp every last detail. Lines

55 – 58, 62 – 66, and 80 – 83 are big picture statements that directly relate to this question. Those kinds of statements are what you want to comprehend during your first read of the text.

12. **H**. First, check out your answers. If you remember the first paragraph a bit, choice H should immediately ring a bell. You may remember the passage mentioning frequent shifts in weather from cold to warm, from storms to droughts, etc. If you do not remember, glance back to the initial paragraph. While you need to keep a good pace, don't rush too much once you get close to finding an answer. While choices G and J appear in the text, they are not the main idea of the paragraph. G is presented as an incorrect view of the Little Ice Age, and J is a small detail, not the main idea.

13. **D**. First of all, you may have been able to eliminate choices B and C, as A and D connect better to the main ideas of the passage. However, whether you eliminated those choices or not, you probably still have to go back to the text to find the one correct answer. This question says exactly where to look (line 28), so glancing back will not cost much time. Again, the key is to not hurry too much when looking back. We are in the right place, and this is not the time to cut corners. By reading the entire thought, lines 24 – 31, we see that these records had a little value, which fits D more than A.

14. **F**. Here is another question in which it is essential to look back to the text. And again, it's necessary to read extra text to get the complete thought. By starting reading at line 47, we see that the events happened during the Little Ice Age. Furthermore, even if you did not understand the complicated sentence in lines 47 – 54, choice F best connects with the biggest theme of this essay: that climate plays some role in history, but does not completely determine it.

15. **A**. This is a common question type in which we must interpret a complicated sentence. As usual, it can be helpful to start reading prior to line 71, although on this question context only helps a bit. In the end, understanding lines 71 – 75 is the key to success. If you missed this question, reread the sentence very slowly and look up any words you do not know. Also note that choice A best fits with the theme of climate affecting world events to some extent – it would be the best guess, even if you did not understand lines 71 – 75. Even questions about small sections relate to the big picture of the essay.

16. **J**. Again, this thought does not end at line 79. Reading past line 79 to line 83 (or even a bit further), gets us the complete thought. Choice J connects to the author's point that these climate shifts did play a role in forming modern Europe. Choice F contrasts with what is said in those lines. G and H do not work with those lines or with the main ideas of the final paragraph.

17. **D**. This would be a tough one to remember, although you may recall that the author used the term "intellectually bankrupt" to refer to the idea of environmental determinism, not as a cause of the Little Ice Age. In addition, choice D just seems to make the least sense of the four options. But if you were not at least 75% sure of the answer, a quick lookup would be necessary (see page 68). The final two paragraphs best fit the subject of this question, so that is where we'll begin our search (the first three paragraphs deal more with describing the weather and the methods used to determine it). While searching, we find that Lines 83 – 85 contain many of the words in our answer choices. After carefully reading that area of the text, D can be confirmed as the answer.

18. G. If you need to look this one up, the key is to start your search with the first paragraph. This question is about the beginnings of the Little Ice Age, and is most likely found near the introduction. Sure enough, lines 5 – 7 confirm G as the correct choice. Of course, the information you need isn't always going to be exactly where expected, but searching smart (see page 73) will help save time.

19. D. We probably want to look this one up, especially since its answer is easy to find. The first paragraph described the weather of the Little Ice Age in detail, and everything we need to answer the question can be found there.

20. G. If you read the passage closely, hopefully this statement stuck out to you. <u>Sometimes ACT asks questions about minor details in the passage, especially when these details are unusual, humorous, or relevant to our current lives.</u> Still, this information could easily be missed during a first read. Unfortunately this question is a tough one to look up efficiently; the answer could fit in many different places in the passage. Simply searching the text for the unusual word "anomaly" is a solid tactic on this question (it appears in line 16).

Note: Stay relaxed, focused, and interested in the passage when first reading it (see pages 59 and 66). You will remember minor, yet interesting details if you are truly attentive to the passage's subject.

Passage III – Humanities

21. C. This passage focused mainly on Armstrong's many contributions to music, and choice C is by far the best expression of this idea. If you missed this one, reread the first paragraph and skim back over the passage. You will find just how well C fits. Note that D is true, but it focuses on a small section of the essay, not the main idea. Choices A and B both contain untrue statements and mention rather unimportant parts of the essay (his emotions and his tone).

22. J. At no point did the author mention any of Armstrong's recordings by name. The essay took a wider approach to his music in general; it did not get into specific recordings. If you wanted to confirm this quickly in the text, that would be OK, but you also must be confident in your reading ability sometimes. You simply do not have the time to look up every single answer in the text.

23. B. Choice B best fits the passage as a whole. Right from the first paragraph – a great place to find general statements about the essay's subject – we see several mentions of Armstrong's incredible improvisational skills. If you were worried about your pace, this would be a good place to cut a corner, immediately go with B, and move on to the next question. B just seems to make the most sense, especially since the other choices mention minor parts of the essay.

24. G. Choice G adequately sums up paragraph two and gives its function in the essay. Choices F and J are small parts of the paragraph and are not even entirely true – only one mentor was identified, and Henderson did not develop the musical style. H did not appear in the paragraph at all; no comparisons are made between the two.

25. C. Ideally, you will know this one based off the first read. Although this question references a rather small part of the essay, ACT often asks questions about interesting facts such as these. Of course, with the pressure of the test, it still is easy to miss this information. If you are searching back, concentrating on first sentences of paragraphs (see page 80) or having a good knowledge of the passage's progression (page 74) both lead you to the correct information quickly.

26. **F.** First, glance at your choices. Choice F may jump out to you, as Armstrong was never characterized as someone who had a "strong desire" to change music. Even knowing this, you may still want to glance at the last paragraph since it will only take a few seconds. Choice G appears in lines 79 – 80 and 84 – 88, H appears in lines 75 – 78, and J appears in lines 74 – 75. Choice F is not in this paragraph.

27. **C.** You may have caught this answer while doing number 26. If not, you simply need to skim the paragraph and find the sentence that matches up to this question (lines 78 – 81).

28. **G.** City names, like all capitalized proper nouns, are easy to find in the text. A common mistake on this question is to pick F because it is the final city mentioned in the passage. When searching back you need to read whole sentences. You cannot choose an answer based on just glancing at a few words (see page 76). Although New Orleans appears last, New York is the place where Armstrong settled (lines 28 – 29).

29. **A.** Glance at the answers, and then head back to the mentioned lines. You may have already been leaning towards choice A – it best fits the characterization of Armstrong in this passage – and that text confirms it. If you had trouble with this one, carefully reread that area in the text. While glissandos, his trumpet, and orchestras are mentioned, choices B, C, and D do not say the same thing that the text says.

30. **H.** Skimming through the paragraph for the words "orchestra" or "swing" would be a good start here. We find them in line 68, but, as usual, we should start reading a bit before that. Reading from the beginning of the quote in line 66, we see that the orchestra does not know they have started to swing. Thus, choice H is true.

Passage IV – Natural Science

31. **C.** You may remember that there was no mention of qi having any sort of temperature. If not, no problem, finding the unusual word "qi" is fairly easy (it's mentioned three times in the first paragraph). Beginning our search there, we find information that matches up to the answer choices in lines 12 – 15. After reading that area it becomes clear that C is the correct choice.

32. **F.** As usual, the *Natural Science* passage starts to get technical. After glancing at the answers, we can head over to lines 35 – 45. As we skim back through the paragraph, the necessary information pops up around lines 39 – 45. Reading those lines very closely (don't cut corners here!), we find that choice F is completely true. The other choices are close, but they just don't match up to the text as well as F does.

33. **C.** Since there is no mention of any of these conditions in the fifth paragraph (or near there), we will have to use some logic to get this one. The study in the fifth paragraph focuses on the medical reasoning to acupuncture's blocking of pain signals. Since headaches are the only option that involves pain, C is the

rational choice. Occasionally, logic is necessary on *Natural Science* questions. More often, however, logic can simply help you guess accurately when you are running low on time. Finally, always be sure to read the question carefully; if you really understand the question here, this one is not too difficult.

34. **J**. First of all, note that this question begins "According to the passage…" This means that the answer is probably going to be in the text somewhere – not much interpretation needed. That said, this is still a tricky question, so let's take it one step at a time. First we need to find the experiment by looking for the name "Cho." Now that we got there, let's look over the experiment's description (lines 55 – 75). If you remember this part (which would be ideal) or are worried about time, you may cheat a bit and skim to the most relevant parts. It appears that two things cause visual cortex activity: exposure to light and stimulating the vision related acupoints. Since we saw in lines 56 – 59 that those acupoints are on the outside of the foot, choice J is correct. Choice G is a common mistake on this question. Carefully reread lines 64 – 72 if you chose G. As always, you must understand the text, not just search for certain words.

Note: Remember that ACT tends to ask about important parts of the passage. They usually are not testing your memory of meaningless facts. In Cho's experiment, the most important finding was that the acupoints on the foot caused stimulation of the visual cortex.

35. **B**. Choice B seems to be an underlying theme to the entire essay: we know a little about the science behind acupuncture, but we still have a lot to learn. If you do need to confirm the answer in the last paragraph, make sure you read the text carefully. Too much skimming will end up costing you more time as you look back and forth between the text and your choices. A careful read of the first two sentences should be enough to prove choice B correct.

36. **J**. Qi seems to be the driving force for all of this Chinese medicine, so J makes sense. However, if you have time to look this one up, just find the word "yin" or "yang" and reread that area.

37. **A**. You may remember that one of these *yins* or *yangs* resulted in hyper kind of conditions (agitation, fast pulse, fever, etc.), while the other resulted in relaxed conditions (pale face, slow pulse, etc.). From that knowledge you could determine that choice A is the odd one out here.

38. **H**. Here is a standard 'vocabulary in context question.' By reading lines 47 – 49 we should be able to figure this one out. If you ever have trouble with this kind of question, at least attempt to eliminate answer choices you know are incorrect. Choices F and J would probably be the first two eliminated on this particular question. Also, when practicing, always look up vocabulary you do not know.

39. **D**. If you really understand Cho's experiment, choice D clearly makes the most sense here. If you didn't quite get it, no worries! Searching around the paragraph about Cho, we find the phrase "placebo effect" in line 78. By reading lines 78 – 80, we can confirm D as the answer.

40. **G**. Glance through the answer choices, and then head to the last paragraph. The opening sentence is the only one that gives the author's opinion, and it matches up well to choice G. The first sentence of a paragraph is always important and should be read carefully.

Test 64E – Reading Answers and Explanations – Look-Back Method

Passage I – Prose Fiction

We begin by doing questions that mention specific line numbers.

5. **C**. The question mentions lines 10 – 13, but it also says "In relation to the first paragraph's…" We might as well read the entire first paragraph, as it will help on the question and give us a nice introduction to the passage. Based on the woman's dream and her general frustration about her situation, it seems that the image of the door that won't open serves to intensify the hopelessness.

9. **C**. From our knowledge of the first paragraph and from reading sentences near line 58, we see that she gets in a bad mood when thinking about other people dreaming. Notice also that C is the only answer choice that sounds good when you substitute it for the word "humor."

Now we look for shorter questions and those that say "According to the passage"

7. **D**. This one is difficult to find, but while skimming through the text we can eliminate some answers and narrow it down. First of all, we can eliminate choice A. Based on our read of the first paragraph, it is clear that the problem is not too much dreaming. We can also eliminate C, as her problem is that she does not dream at all. Finally, looking at the dialogue in the passage, it appears that the narrator is a helpful person, so B can be eliminated. Thus, choice D must be correct. We can confirm this by reading lines 31 – 34.

8. **J**. This one also is not easy to find, but if we use the tactic of reading the first sentence of each paragraph (see page 81), we run into the answer. The sentence beginning at line 52 mentions the woman trying to dream the narrators dream. She does this "with the lights out, hiding." Thus, J is the correct answer. Notice also that choices F, G, and H don't seem to fit the character of the woman (she is not "powerful," "playful," or "confident" anywhere in this passage).

4. **J**. We already saw the door in the first paragraph. Rereading that area, it is clear that the door that won't open matches up with the woman being unable to dream. This answer also just seems to make sense with everything we have seen so far.

10. **H**. Searching for the capitalized name "Kafka," we run into it in line 63. Now we must interpret that area of the text (lines 61 – 64). The narrator compliments Kafka on his ability to tell dreams without making them rational, so H is the only answer that matches the text.

6. **G**. Searching for the unusual word "amniotic," we find it in the first sentence of the paragraph at line 71. The text says this dream is "the one she likes best," so it is hard to argue with G. If time allowed us to confirm the answer, reading further through that paragraph proves G is correct. Answers F, H, and J simply are not supported by the text.

Now that we got the easier ones out of the way, we try the remaining questions

1. **B**. First of all, let's eliminate choice A as a possible answer. We have seen a few times already that the one woman cannot dream, so this must be incorrect. Next, we can remove C. This makes it sound like there is an outside narrator who knows everyone's thoughts. Based on the facts we've picked up, the narrator is one of the two characters, and it doesn't appear that she knows the other woman's thoughts (other than the things the woman tells her). Now, looking back to the text, we find that choice B fits better than D. The narrator only gives "detailed narration" of one of her dreams, not "several" of them.

2. **F**. We can eliminate choices G and J fairly quickly based on a quick look over of the passage. At no point is the narrator "uninterested" or "angry"; she actually seems concerned and interested in helping the woman. Now, to pick between F and H, let's look at the descriptions of the woman. Looking at her quotes in lines 14 – 16 and line 51, it seems like "frustrated" fits a little better than "resigned." Also, the description of the narrator in F is more accurate.

3. **B**. Choice B just seems to fit everything we have read so far (the 'big picture'), but we can also confirm this one in the text. Lines 2 – 4, 25 – 30, and 58 – 61 all point to "self-awareness" as the correct answer.

Note: Questions that say the words "it can reasonably be inferred" are usually best to do near the end.

Passage II – Social Science

We will start with question 12, then move to the 'line number' questions (12 mentions the first paragraph, which is a good place to begin).

12. **H**. After we read this paragraph closely, H emerges as the best answer. Choices F and G were presented as incorrect ways to look at the Little Ice Age (lines 1 – 7). J is true, but it is a small detail, not the main idea of the paragraph.

13. **D**. This thought seems to begin in line 22 and end in line 31 (read the entire thought! – see page 82). Reading closely, we can interpret that text to say, 'In the past, people like John Evelyn kept weather records. The records have value in extreme cases, but ultimately are not very accurate or specific.' "The worst rain storm in memory" would be one of those records that is only of limited value, so choice D is correct.

14. **F**. Try to simplify the text in lines 47 – 54 without getting bogged down by the somewhat difficult vocabulary. Here's one way we can break down that sentence: 'The Little Ice Age occurred during centuries that included many important European events.' Thus, these events "took place during the Little Ice Age." There is nothing in that area of the text saying the events were caused or not caused by the Little Ice Age, so the other options are incorrect.

15. **A**. Let's begin reading at line 66 (the beginning of the thought), but still focus most on 71 – 75, as that is the statement we are interpreting. Reading those lines closely, we can interpret the text to say – 'weather made a large difference in the amount of food available, which caused differences in people's

behavior. The change in behavior affected entire continents over many decades.' This matches up directly to choice A. Choice D is close, but just doesn't fit as well with everything else we have read so far (the big picture).

16. **J**. On this question we certainly must read past line 79, as nearly any answer (except perhaps G) could make sense at that point. In fact, reading the whole paragraph is not a bad idea. Now, looking back between our answers and the final paragraph, we can begin to eliminate choices. F is wrong, as the exact opposite is said in lines 80 – 81. Choice G does not have much in common with lines 77 – 79 or the last paragraph in general, so it is wrong. H is harder to eliminate, but lines 86 – 88 do prove it incorrect. Choice J makes sense given the commentary in lines 80 – 83, and is the correct choice.

After the line numbers, we move to the shorter, simpler questions

20. **G**. Questions about general, preliminary facts often are found in the first paragraph. Indeed, the last sentence of the first paragraph plainly gives the answer to this question. Searching for the unusual word "anomaly" would be another method to solve this one. See pages 79 and 80 for more on these tactics.

Note: Don't get too stubborn. If you can't find an answer for a while, take a guess and move on.

18. **G**. Again, this general fact appears in the first paragraph. Furthermore, try to pay attention to everything you read (see page 81); we have already seen this sentence while working on other questions.

17. **D**. You may remember seeing this when doing question 16. The "food crises" mentioned in the question appear in the first sentence of the last paragraph. In that paragraph, lines 83 – 86 confirm D as the correct answer. If you did not know where to find this answer, searching for the many long words in the answer choices would lead you to the correct information quickly.

19. **D**. This question about a general fact is answered in the first paragraph (as usual). The "unusually calm ocean" is the only element that is not listed. Again, these answer choices also contain words that are easily found in the text.

Finally, we get to the only big picture question for this passage

11. **A**. We have seen this idea a few times by now: climate change made a difference in history, but it was not the only factor. This is most plainly said in the last paragraph, which is a common place to find big picture conclusions.

Passage III – Humanities

We begin by doing the questions that mention specific line numbers or paragraphs.

24. **G**. While choices F and J did appear in the text, G gives the main function of the paragraph as a whole: a rundown of Armstrong's first years in the business.

Note: It may be helpful to skim or read the first paragraph when doing this question. It is OK to take extra time to get background information about the passage, characters, etc. if necessary (see page 83).

27. **C**. Reading through the final paragraph (with this question in mind), we find in line 80 that Armstrong wanted to promote the sense of pleasure that music gave him.

26. **F**. Again, let's carefully read through the last paragraph with this question in mind. We first eliminate choice J because of lines 74 – 75. Next we eliminate H because of lines 75 – 78. Lastly, we get rid of choice G, as that appears in lines 84 – 88. Armstrong was an incredible musician, but nothing in that paragraph says he had "a desire to reshape American music," so F is correct.

29. **A**. Let's get the whole thought by looking at lines 44 – 57. This text clearly gives evidence of Armstrong's amazing skill as a musician. Furthermore, in lines 53 – 57 he didn't invent the glissando or use a different trumpet – he just played very, very well.

30. **H**. The percussionist says the orchestra swings "without them even knowing it" in lines 67 – 68.

Now to the shorter questions and answers, which are usually easy to look up

28. **G**. Let's search the text for the cities, as capitalized words are easy to find. Paragraph two contains three of these cities, so let's read it closely (remember, you are close to a correct answer, don't go too fast and mess it up!). The last sentence says he "finally settled in New York," so G must be correct. New Orleans does appear in the final paragraph, but it does not say anything about him moving back there.

23. **B**. This answer is tough to find, as this is more of a big picture question. We cannot pick questions in perfect order, though, so let's try it anyway. By reading first sentences of paragraphs and other pieces of the essay (not too much skimming), we can quickly eliminate choices A and C; they are unimportant parts of the passage. Choice D isn't bad, but the "emphasis on improvisation" is a major theme presented in lines 5 – 12 (the first paragraph is a great place to find big picture information!). It also is mentioned in lines 40 – 43.

Now that we finished the 'line-number' and shorter questions, we complete the remaining three questions

25. **C**. Some of these answers may sound familiar, as we saw them while completing question 29. So, let's head back to the paragraph we used on that question (lines 44 – 57). In lines 51 – 53 we see choices A, B, and D. Choice C is not found anywhere in the passage.

Note: If you did not recognize these answers from question 29, you could easily find the necessary information anyway. The first sentence of the fourth paragraph talks about "superhuman feats." That certainly matches up with the subject of this question (see page 81 for more on first sentences).

22. **J**. While this question seems to focus on small details, a solid understanding of the big picture (which hopefully we are starting to get!) would save a lot of time. Choices F, G, and H all fit the passage's focus on Armstrong being an innovator who changed jazz and music in general. Choice J almost fits, but this passage took a more general approach and did not get into specific recordings. Questions like this are difficult when using the Look-Back method, but try your best to logic them out. Also make sure you don't get too stubborn; it is easy to spend too much time on questions like this one.

21. **C**. Choice C is the best option for several reasons. First of all, it makes sense given the text we have read so far, especially the first paragraph (where the main idea is often established). Secondly, the other options all have some flaw. "The narrow emotional range" and "recorded masterpieces" do not appear anywhere in this passage, and his tone is mentioned only as a minor detail. Choice C is the only option that truly captures the focus of the passage.

Passage IV – Natural Science

We begin by doing the questions that mention specific line numbers or paragraphs

33. **C**. This question is tricky, as none of these conditions are mentioned specifically in that paragraph, and looking at nearby paragraphs does not help either. In line 44 the process is said to block pain signals, though. Headaches are the only option that involves pain. Occasionally, a little logic is necessary on *Natural Science* questions. Also, logic can help you make accurate guesses when time is running low.

38. **H**. This is a difficult one to figure out in context, so we will have to rely on our vocabulary and possibly a little science knowledge. The sentence is saying that the acupoints are in spots where a bunch of nerves are clustered together.

35. **B**. Reading through the last paragraph carefully, we see that the study "raises more questions than it answers," but also "demonstrated new functional effects of acupuncture." Choices A and D are clearly too one-sided, and choice C is wrong because the methods of previous studies were not questioned.

40. **G**. Again this question simply requires careful reading and interpretation of the text. The first sentence of the paragraph gives the answer. Read it closely if you missed this one.

Now we go to shorter questions and those that say "According to the passage..."

34. **J**. Finding Cho's study is relatively easy, as a search for the name "Cho" finds that he only appears in the right-hand column. If time permitted, it would be worth reading about his entire experiment (lines 55 – 80), so we understand the whole background to this question. If time does not permit, we can concentrate on lines 67 – 75, which give the causes of increased visual cortex activity: a flash of light and

stimulation of a vision-related acupoint. This eliminates choices F and G. Searching around this area of the text, we find that the acupoints were on the outside of the foot (lines 57 – 59). The big toe is a nonacupoint (line 79).

39. **D**. If you had time to carefully read about the experiment while doing #34, choice D may have jumped out to you (remember that extra reading helps on later questions!). If you didn't get this one right away, a search through Cho's experiment for the unusual word "placebo" leads to the needed information.

Note: Choice D also just makes the most sense. Logic tells us that lights, eye charts, and vision-related things would naturally increase visual activity in the brain. They would not be considered placebo effects. Sometimes logic and rational thought can help on the *Natural Science* passage.

36. **J**. Searching for the unusual words "yin" and "yang" in the text would be a good way to attack this question (they are found in the third paragraph). Reading that paragraph carefully, we see that shortages or excesses of qi cause problems and upset balance of yin and yang.

37. **A**. Looking right back at the yin and yang paragraph, lines 30 – 31 clearly give the answer.

31. **C**. We just saw that shortages and excesses of qi cause problems, so choices A and B are incorrect. Now let's look to the first paragraph since qi is mentioned there several times. Lines 12 – 15 say that disturbing the flow of qi can cause problems, so "a change in temperature" must be the correct answer.

Note that this particular Natural Science passage has no big picture questions

Test 64E – Science Answers and Explanations

Passage I

1. **D**. Figure 1 is mentioned, so that is the first place to look. This is an odd looking figure, but, as always, everything is labeled. The most usable piece of information given in the question is the number 125°. Looking at Figure 1, it would make sense that 125° would fall between the line marked 103° and the line marked 142°. This area is labeled as a shadow zone with no p or s waves.

2. **G**. As always, the key to this question is to pay close attention to the labels and keys involved with the figure. P-waves are solid lines (see key). The mantle is the white area around the core (labeled in figure). The core is the inner two circles of the figure (labeled). We can clearly see two p-waves travel through the mantle into the core. Choices F, H, and J simply are not true. Note that the word "refracted" is defined in the text, although you do not need to know its meaning to get this question right.

3. **D**. Go to Figure 3. We are told to look at the time of p-waves and s-waves 10,500 km away. Distances are found on the X (horizontal) axis, and time is on the Y (vertical) axis. Now plot where the p and s waves would be at 10,500 km (this number is slightly off the chart, so estimate where 10,500 would be if the chart continued). The p-waves would be between 13 and 14 minutes, and the s-waves look to be around 25 minutes (again, the chart must be extended). The waves are more than 10 minutes apart.

Note: Always pay close attention to the scale when plotting points that are off the chart. For example, on Figure 3 each 1,000 km is only about 1.5 centimeters long. 10,500 km would be a very short distance away from 10,000 km.

4. **F**. By looking at the axes we get an idea of exactly what Figure 3 is representing. It is displaying how long it takes a seismograph to get a reading based on how many kilometers it is from the earthquake. It is logical that the graph will be at 0 km, 0 min just as the earthquake hits: the seismograph has not had any time to get a reading yet. As usual, the scientific word *seismograph* is defined in the text. An additional explanation of Figure 3 is found in the text as well. Remember that the text can help if you are confused by a question or cannot decipher a graph or table (see page 95).

5. **A**. On this question, you could look for the word *amplitude* in the text, but it's not there. Harder questions occasionally require that you know some basic science concepts (see page 98). The amplitude is simply the height of the wave from top to bottom. Figure 2 clearly shows that s-waves have a larger amplitude.

Passage II

6. **F**. Looking at Figure 2, we see that "lake clay" is the light gray area. The line labeled Winnipeg has the thinnest amount of lake clay.

7. **C**. Looking at Figure 3, we see the X axis is labeled on top as $S^{18}O$. It also says that smaller values are toward the left side of the graph. The dots that are furthest to the left occur between 20 and 30 m depth (Y axis).

8. **J**. As we move from the far right of Figure 2 (labeled Grand Forks) to the line labeled Site 3, the lake clay thickens. At the same time the glacial till (the striped area) decreases in thickness.

9. **C**. We need to find the elevation of the top of the glacial till at each of the three sites. At Site 1, the striped area stops at around 200 m elevation (use the Y axis). The area stops slightly higher in Site 2, and a bit lower in site 3. Thus, graph C correctly presents the information.

10. **J**. They give us a complicated sounding question here, but once we break it down, it actually proves to be fairly simple. The question mentions Figure 3, tells us that the water soaks up to 3 meters below the surface, and asks for the $S^{18}O$. The first step is to plot the 3 meters on the Y axis for depth. Now we just need a reading for $S^{18}O$. On all three graphs the plotted dots are reading roughly -15 for depths of around 3 meters.

Passage III

11. **B**. This clearly is not a 'graph question,' so let's look to the text. Read the information given for Experiment 3, and skim the text in the beginning of the passage to get a basic understanding of the experiment. We do not find a direct answer to the question, so we have to use some logic. Choices A, C, and D do not make much sense. It seems to reason that an aluminum bottle would roll faster than plastic, contain as much liquid as you wanted (you could always get a bigger bottle!), and be less likely to break than plastic. Furthermore, the text for Experiment 3 mentions that looking at the bubbles in the bottle was part of the experiment. Thus, B makes the most sense. See page 96 for more on this kind of logic based question.

12. **J**. We simply need to match up numbers in the "before shaking" columns of Table 1 and Table 2. Trials 1, 3, and 5 all read 1.75 seconds. Answer J is the only correct choice. Note that when the text mentions "the results of Experiments 1 and 2" it is usually referring to the charts below the Experiments' descriptions.

13. **D**. First we look towards Experiment 2. Using the labels in the table, we can clearly find the before and after shaking times. It appears that shaking the can adds a fraction of a second to the roll time. Note that choices A and B do not make sense logically and should be immediately ignored.

14. **H**. This is a somewhat difficult question, but there are a couple of different ways to solve it. First of all, let's look at Trial 5. The numbers in the table probably are not enough to reach an answer, so let's move into the text. The next to last sentence of Experiment 2's description provides helpful information about Trial 5. Looking to our answer choices, G and H seem to make the most sense, as those choices mention the "two hours" we also saw in Trial 5's description. But which one is correct? Well, remember that **all of these experiments are based off actual scientific trials. ACT will not give you bogus information that contradicts common sense.** If you have ever shaken a bottle of pop, you probably are

aware that the bubbles do not last for over 2 hours. Thus, choice H makes more sense than G. Additionally, the last sentence under Experiment 3 and the "before shaking" time of Trial 3 provide further evidence for choice H.

Note (important!): This question becomes much easier if you truly understand the design and goals of the experiment. When you run into a question like this one, take a little time to figure out what is happening in the experiment.

15. **A**. This question uses much of the same information we found while completing number 14. In Experiment 2, the before shaking roll time was measured at 1.75 seconds after a two hour wait (see the data and description for Trial 5). The students are following the same procedure, so there is no reason to think the roll time would surpass 1.86 seconds. In fact, the time would probably just be 1.75 seconds again. **Don't overthink it; these questions are easier than they look!**

16. **H**. In Trial 3, the beverage had not been shaken at all, and the before shaking roll time was 1.75 seconds. In Trial 4, 15 minutes after shaking the can, the before shaking roll time was 1.86 seconds. In Trial 5, after waiting 2 hours, the before shaking time was 1.75 seconds again. So, the time was affected at 15 minutes, but not at two hours. Sometime in between 15 minutes and 2 hours the bubbles stopped affecting roll time. This difficult kind of question is common towards the end of passages; we must understand the question, read some text, and interpret data to get the correct answer.

Passage IV

17. **A**. In Figure 1 we find absorption as the Y (vertical) Axis. Chlorophyll *b* is the solid line, and it reaches its greatest absorption number around a wavelength of 480 nm. Heading up to Table 1, we find that the color with a wavelength of 480 nm is blue.

18. **F**. The first step here is to look in the text to find information directly relating to this question. Unfortunately, we do not find any, as this is a 'real science question' (page 98). However, the passage mentions chlorophyll a few times, so "chloroplasts" is a logical choice, even if you have limited knowledge about cells and photosynthesis. Note that the parts of a cell have shown up in 'real science questions' on a few ACTs over the last five years.

19. **B**. First, plot each of the options carefully on Figure 2. 430 nm has the highest value for rate of photosynthesis. It is the only value higher than the rate at 670 nm.

20. **G**. Here is another example of a 'real science question.' As instructed in the question, look to the chemical equation. It looks like the carbon becomes part of $C_6H_{12}O_6$ – which is the chemical formula for a basic type of sugar. However, even if you didn't know about $C_6H_{12}O_6$ you may know that sugar is generated from photosynthesis. Since this passage focuses on photosynthesis, "sugar" is the logical choice. Always remember to think and use basic logic, even on 'real science questions.'

21. **C**. This is a common two-chart question. We need to get some information from Figure 2 and then apply it on Figure 1. Looking at Figure 2, we see that the wavelength with the highest rate of

photosynthesis is 440 nm (use the axes). We carry that to Figure 1, as that chart gives information on absorption (again, axes are the key). Paying attention to the scale on the X axis, we plot the 440 nm. It appears to be the wavelength where chlorophyll *a* hits its relative absorption peak.

Passage V

22. **G**. This question requires a chart lookup and a little logic to complete. First, we go to Table 1 (the primary source of data for Experiment 1). Although there is not a liquid labeled as "ethanol," we can assume that Liquid 1 is pure ethanol. Why? Liquid 1 contains 0 grams of H_2O; the entire mass is made up of ethanol. This is the kind of basic logic that is used on many ACT Science questions.

23. **C**. This question mentions all three experiments, so it's important to solve it one step at a time. The only place we see "PA-11" is in Table 3, so we will begin there. First, let's read the description so we can interpret exactly what Table 3 is showing. Now that we have that information, we move forward. The question asks for a density reading, which we find in the tables under Experiments 1 and 2. So, we have to find a way to connect the chart involving "PA-11" with the charts that give density readings. As usual, the axes and labels are the key. Notice how Liquids 1 – 10 appear in all 3 charts. This will be our connector. "PA-11" sunk in Liquid 5, but rose in Liquid 6. Thus, its density is most likely between those recorded for Liquid 5 (.999 – see Table 1) and Liquid 6 (1.05 – see Table 2).

24. **H**. Go to Experiment 2. "Mass of solution in graduated cylinder" is the third column. Plot where 67.54 g would be in that column (it will end up just off the chart). Now let's figure out the density. It looks like as mass increases, density increases slightly. Thus, choice H fits the pattern.

25. **B**. Looking at Experiment 3, we never see R's come before S's. All the other choices make sense given the data in the chart. Some basic knowledge about density would also be helpful here.

26. **F**. First, let's take a second to figure out what is happening in Experiments 1 and 2. From the descriptions and tables, we see that the students are putting different amounts of liquids together and finding the density and mass of each combination. It would make sense to tare the scale (reset it to 0.000 g) so the cylinder's mass is not included in the measurement. This would make it easier to simply find the mass of the added liquids, which seems to be the goal. This question requires logical thinking based on the goals of the experiment. The answer is not directly presented in the text (see page 96).

27. **B**. Here you have to know a bit about density. A simple explanation is that denser things stay at the bottom of a liquid, while less dense things rise to the top. So, choice B fits the data and makes scientific sense. Note that choices C and D do not agree with the data in Table 3. Even if you were unsure about the rules of density, these choices could be proven wrong by carefully reading the chart.

Passage VI

28. **H**. Remember that Experiment 1 includes all the information until Experiment 2 begins. So, as usual, we start by looking in the chart (Table 1). In Table 1, Species B and D have plus signs under at least one

of the Lactose columns. ACT does not directly try to trick you – we can assume these plus signs mean that the species fermented lactose.

29. **C**. This is another question that requires a mixture of interpreting the charts and logic. Table 2 shows similar data to what we saw in Table 1, except that now combinations of species are used. While we cannot get an answer purely from Table 2, we can use Table 1 to understand these species combinations a little better. Comparing the charts, it appears that each combination has a plus sign at every place the individual species have pluses. In fact, sometimes extra pluses are added as well (see "B and D" or "C and D"). So, since Species C has pluses in both sucrose columns, and Species B has pluses in both lactose columns, their combination will have pluses in every column.

30. **G**. ACT gives us a long, complicated sounding question, but, as usual, it is easier than it looks. The question basically just said that nothing happened in the sucrose, but both acid and CO_2 were produced in the lactose. Species B, which has minuses under the sucrose columns and pluses under the lactose columns, fits this description perfectly.

31. **D**. This question applies a lot of the logic we used to answer # 29. We need to compare the individual results for Species C and D (Table 1) to the combined results of Species C and D (Table 2). Choice D is the only option that gives a true statement. It would also help to know the definition of "synergism," which is found in the text. Carefully reading the text can be helpful when a word or question confuses you (see page 95).

32. **G**. This question is not solvable purely from the charts or pictures, so we must move to the text. The paragraph just above Table 1 provides the information we need. Using the guidelines listed, we see that Species D in sucrose would turn yellow (plus sign under the acid column), but would not form a gas bubble (minus sign under the CO_2 column).

Note: It can be a bit difficult to find the correct information necessary to solve this problem, but you can be sure it is in the passage somewhere. ACT would not expect you to know something this specific or advanced without help from the data.

33. **D**. Again, we must know and understand the definition of "synergism" to solve this question. *Synergism* means that the combination of the two species' results (Table 2) has greater effects than the sum of each individual species' results (Table 1). Since the combination of Species A and C has no more pluses than Species C does by itself, there was not any synergism. Note that choices B and C are simply not consistent with the data given in Table 2.

Passage VII – The Conflicting Viewpoint Passage (7 Questions)

34. **H**. This is a somewhat difficult question to begin with; do not hesitate to take some extra time reading and familiarizing yourself with the passage if necessary. The DNA Hypothesis says that the amount of DNA is correlated with the number of chromosomes, so choices H and J make sense. Since the DNA Hypothesis does not give direct information on where chromosomes are found, we can look to

the introductory information for help. There it mentions that chromosomes are found only in the nucleus (the picture also clearly shows this).

35. D. This question looks complicated, but it's really just asking, "Which of these things are found only in the nucleus?" The introductory text plainly states that chromosomes are found only in the nucleus. Always try to break down and simplify Science Test questions. They usually are easier than they look (see page 89).

36. J. The introductory text clearly states that both proteins and DNA consist of subunits. None of the other choices are supported by the passage.

Note: When the question says "According to the passage" it usually is referring to the introductory information, not the hypotheses.

37. A. While we may not fully understand why choice A is "strong evidence," the fact is, we don't really need to understand it. Choice A is the only option that mentions something expressly said in the Protein Hypothesis. B, C and D simply do not appear in that hypothesis.

38. F. This question is not as difficult as it looks. It is lengthy, but we could break it down to – 'Genes have been found in the cytoplasm outside the nucleus. Which hypothesis does this contradict?' The rest of the question has little to do with the information presented in the passage and can be ignored. The most logical answer is choice F. The DNA Hypothesis says genes are made of DNA, and DNA is only in the nucleus. Since this question says genes were found outside of the nucleus, we have a contradiction.

39. B. In the third sentence of the DNA Hypothesis the scientist uses this fact to support his argument. Choices A, C, and D are never said in the DNA Hypothesis (choice A is almost said, but read closely to notice a small but significant difference).

40. J. In the introduction we find the sentence, "DNA consists of subunits called *nucleotides*." Amino Acids are mentioned, but they are grouped with the proteins, and have no connection to the DNA. Thus, choice J, the chain of nucleotides, is the correct option.

Note: This ACT Science Test had a few particularly difficult passages, so don't worry if you did not do as well as you would've liked. Keep reviewing this book, taking practice tests, and learning from your mistakes; you will quickly see improvement in your Science Test score.